Dessau's book is a must-read for anyone who wants to avoid muddling through their job and career. It provides proven and practical advice anchored in Nigel's twenty-five-years-plus career as a successful manager and leader."

Don Ruse, Partner at Axiom Consulting Partners

—⸺⸺—

People get stuck in their careers, both in smaller organizations as well as within large ones. The book contains very sage advice that I really believe will be a helpful guide for people trying to grow to the next step. Even long-time managers who find themselves in marketplaces that are changing rapidly around them—like my own crazy industry—will benefit from the discussions. Change management is often required in these circumstances, and you can definitely be trapped if you don't recognize the need for new approaches and new management and leadership styles.

Lois Paul, Founder, President and
CEO of Lois Paul and Partners

—⸺⸺—

Become a 21ˢᵗ Century Executive features some great leadership advice from someone who has been there, done that (and done it well). This new book by Nigel Dessau is a powerful tool for those who want to advance their careers and rise to the top of the heap. Nigel lays out a solid framework that helps the reader make better career-impacting decisions. It should be on every leader's desk!

Kent Hoffman, CMO at BearCom Wireless

—⸺⸺—

Nigel's twenty-five-year marketing career unearths the definable difference between leadership and management—a must-read for anyone with the desire to build effective teams.

Having worked with Nigel and seen his *3 Minute Mentoring* in practice, his practical approach will free up more time for strategic and creative development—paramount for any business leader.

Nigel is one of the more forward-thinking and visionary marketing leaders in tech—a terrific guide to success!

Mark Bunting, Visiting Professor of High-Tech Advertising and Marketing, University of Texas

Nigel Dessau, with whom I worked closely at IBM for years, has written a very interesting book on a long neglected subject: how do you succeed in middle management? CEOs and other senior executives deal with big issues—leadership, strategy, transformation, survival—and lots of books have been written to help them succeed at these big tasks. The reason that CEOs can focus on the big issues is that they delegate the mundane, everyday ones to their middle managers. And while not as weighty or sexy, the myriad everyday decisions that middle managers make are key factors in the success or failure of their companies, their teams, and their own careers. In the end, how well we [move] through these middle management decisions will often determine whether we get to make bigger ones. *Become a 21ˢᵗ Century Executive: Breaking Away from the Pack* was written for the middle manager, especially those aiming to successfully move up or on. This long-neglected, often derided segment finally has a book of its own.

Irving Wladawsky-Berger, Former IBM Executive and Visiting Lecturer, MIT

While some succeed [at their careers] and others go down in flames, the vast majority get stuck. If you want to know what to do when you get stuck, you should read *Become a 21ˢᵗ Century Executive*. It is realistic, [it is] based on real-life experiences, and it will allow you to unstick yourself and get back to rising to the top.

Andrew Willis, CEO at Stop Abuse Campaign

—◁ɯɯ₰₥ɯ▷—

Middle-management roles are some of the most difficult in any organization. The intersection of strategy and execution creates a unique set of challenges and pressure. Nigel's advice can help leaders become more effective in these critical roles. Navigating the midsection of an organization can be challenging and filled with frustration.

Nigel helps unlock some of this frustration with his timely and relevant advice. Career support to middle managers is lacking in many organizations.

Nigel provides practical insight for leaders to apply to a broad range of critical situations.

Allen Sockwell, CEO, Sockwell Advisors

—◁ɯɯ₰₥ɯ▷—

Dessau has filled in the gap between the MBA degree and the lessons learnt from the school of hard knocks. He has shown us the human side of being a manager by providing a practical, here's-how-to-do-it guide. The observations he makes ring too true in my ears! I wish he had written this book years ago when I started on my career. Thanks, Nigel. You will be a savior to many a [middle] manager.

Robinson Roe, Managing Director Australia
and New Zealand, Air Watch

—◁ɯɯ₰₥ɯ▷—

I wish Nigel had written this book twenty years earlier! His message is particularly poignant to the tech industry executive. The peaks and valleys of tech often create the impression within management that they are solely responsible for the peaks and unjustly blamed for the valleys. Nigel appropriately states that we are accountable for our own success and recognition. And more importantly, he provides us with tools to inspect our performance, our expectations, and our fears. I will make *Become a 21st Century Executive* required reading for my children, employees, and clients.

Mark Ward, Managing Partner, WardCapital

⸺

I highly recommend *Become a 21st Century Executive* wherever you are in your career. You'll find real value across a range of important business topics in virtually no time.

Carmen O'Shea, Head of Talent Marketing &
Interim Head of Diversity at SAP

⸺

With short and thoughtful insight into everything it takes to succeed in middle management, Nigel Dessau helps his readers chart a fast path to the top.

Peter Bingaman, Vice President Marketing and
Communications at MSC Industrial Supply

⸺

I highly recommend keeping a copy of *Become a 21st Century Executive* on your desk. Nigel was the first senior executive to give me a shot at management. Over the year I worked for him, he taught me many of these management lessons. Now readers can have and reference his invaluable advice anytime.

Larkin Kay, Founder at Larkin Kay Marketing

⸺

The *3 Minute Mentor* website succeeded in delivering both new information to the beginning manager and reminders to the experienced manager in a concise, informative, and interesting way. I highly recommend *Become a 21st Century Executive* for anyone in management, regardless of the level. *Become a 21st Century Executive* provides tremendous insight across a range of important business topics.

Ron Greenberg, CEO, rsg.nyc

Finally, a practical guide to helping middle managers not only survive, but thrive in today's complex workplace. *Become a 21st Century Executive* provides sage advice that helps its readers assess their strengths and weaknesses and offers sensible recommendations to address a wide range of workplace situations. I had the pleasure of working for Nigel while we were both at IBM and have seen him drive exceptional results by practicing what he preaches.

Joe Labriola, Vice President of Product Marketing at PGi

Business as usual isn't cutting it anymore. Change, adapt or die is the new mantra for management. Stay ahead of the pack by reading *Become a 21st Century Executive*. Learn from the experience of others as you adapt and change throughout your career.

Jeffrey Hayzlett Global Business Celebrity, TV Commentator, Best-Selling Author, and Sometime Cowboy

Become a 21ˢᵗ Century Executive

Breaking Away from the Pack

NIGEL DESSAU

∞ INFINITY
PUBLISHING

Disclaimer: In all but one case, the names of the people in the case studies in this book are made up, as are their roles. The titles and roles of the people do not match the original situations described. If anyone I know can see themselves in these stories, it is purely coincidental.

Cover art by: © Skypixel | Dreamstime.com

Become a 21st Century Executive: Breaking Away from the Pack
Copyright © 2015 by Nigel Dessau

ISBN 978-1-4958-0082-5 Softcover
ISBN 978-1-4958-0083-2 Hardcover
ISBN 978-1-4958-0084-9 Hour Audio
ISBN 978-1-4958-0085-6 eBook

Published April 2015

INFINITY PUBLISHING
1094 New DeHaven Street, Suite 100
West Conshohocken, PA 19428-2713
Toll-free (877) BUY BOOK
Local Phone (610) 941-9999
Fax (610) 941-9959
Info@buybooksontheweb.com
www.buybooksontheweb.com

DEDICATION

To those who have mentored me over the years: my family, my work colleagues, my friends — but most of all, my wife, Laurie.

Thank you.

Contributors

Author: Nigel Dessau
www.3minutementor.com

Writing Assistance: Joanne Sammer
www.joannesammer.com

Editing: Dr. Tim Morrison
www.writechoiceservices.com

Book Cover and Interior Design: Vanessa Lowry
www.connect4leverage.com

TABLE OF CONTENTS

INTRODUCTION

Stuck in the Middle

In a World of Middle Management

In my career, I have told two bosses that I was going to resign and leave the company. In both cases, what I remember most is the look of fear in both of my managers' eyes when I told them the news. The fear was not caused by my resignation. The fear was there because neither one knew how to handle the situation.

In one case, my manager simply said, "Do you know how this will make me look?" Needless to say, I resisted the urge to blurt out the next thought that came into my mind.

The manager in the other situation merely looked at me blankly. It was clear he had no idea what to do next. To help him out, I suggested that I would go back to my office, start clearing up, and stop responding to e-mail. In the meantime, my manager could call the Human Resources team to find out the next steps. He thanked me and put the call in to HR.

Now, both of these guys were smart and successful. One even had "Senior" in front of his Vice President title. The problem was that with all the training and education these managers had been given, they had little skill or knowledge when it came to dealing with situations like this.

If you have worked in any large organization, a story like this will not be new to you. You often see people who have lots of "smarts" but don't appear to know what they are doing.

A LACK OF TRAINING

Oscar Wilde, the Irish poet and dramatist, once said, "Experience is the name we give to our mistakes." But there are better ways to learn than just failing. So, as Plautus said, "He gains wisdom in a happy way who gains it by another's experience."[1] Well, not making your own mistakes and learning from the mistakes of others would seem to be a better approach.

In this book, we will refer to middle managers as "Stuck-in-the-Middle Managers" *if they plod through life and career struggling, making mistakes, and being unempowered.* Such individuals do not learn from people who have made mistakes. Nor do they learn from their own mistakes. As they start to move up and attain higher levels of responsibility on the job, their tendencies negatively impact not only their own careers, but those of their teammate(s).

By contrast, "21st Century Executives" are people who do not let things simply "happen" to them. They learn from those around them, and they also learn from their own mistakes. They commit to doing things the right way. They take ownership. They demonstrate presence. Empowerment. Integrity. Transparency. They keep the needs of their company and their team at the forefront.

The number of people who tell others that they got where they got with "no plan" always surprises me. They say this as if it were advice they believe others should follow. A 21st Century Executive will not do this.

---

1. Plautus (Titus Maccius Plautus), *Mercatorn* (IV, 7, 40)

SURVIVAL OF THE FITTEST

In life, many move up without planning. Some can even get by on luck but, as they say, "Luck is not a strategy."

What is worse is that we sometimes accept roles or tasks on the assumption that we will be able to "make it up as we go along." We desperately hope that we will figure out what we are doing.

I know. I have done it in my career, once while serving as a senior manager at IBM, and again as a senior vice president at the now-defunct Sun Microsystems.

I was having a great career at IBM. After a slow start, it looked like promotions were coming my way. Then it all stopped. I had failed to understand the organizational changes that were happening around me. A lack of organizational savvy left me exposed without a role and without anyone supporting me. My network was insufficient and my influencing skills weak. Yes, people loved to work with me and said nice things about me — but my career was going nowhere. In short, *I was stuck in the middle,* not really knowing what to do or how to act, and becoming ineffectual.

In the end, I had to accept a role that some considered a step backwards before I could rebuild the credibility, content, approach, and network necessary to restart my progress upwards. While I received a lot of training at IBM, no one had prepared me for this situation.

Some years later, I was working for a company called StorageTek Corporation that was acquired by Sun Microsystems. The team at Sun offered me a role when the acquisition was complete, and I accepted. The culture of Sun was young and exciting, but the management team was unrealistic about the difficulties involved in executing their plans.

I remember one specific project that was being driven from the top. Like most people at the company, I struggled with the project. While we all agreed on the importance of the project in principle, in practice the solution made no sense. Instead of fixing the situation, everyone just plodded along—sticking their heads in the sand—in the hope that someone else would take responsibility and make it work. Not surprisingly, the project failed, and in the end, so did Sun.

Sun was full of amazing and smart people who often lacked the middle-management skills necessary to ensure success. Sun's people were mostly engineers, whereas IBMers tended to be product and sales people—and that is where both companies focused their skill development. *No one questioned how managers would obtain the knowledge and skills necessary to survive middle management and move up to the head table.*

These companies are not unusual. Many companies take a survival-of-the-fittest approach to middle management. *Hence, if you don't learn some basic rules, it is hard to rise above the pack and stand out. Both your business and your career may depend on your learning these roles, but who will teach you?*

THE 3 *MINUTE MENTOR* BEGINS

Like most middle and senior managers, I travel a lot. Bad weather on one trip left me stuck at Dallas-Fort Worth International Airport. To use the time profitably, I browsed the airport bookshop looking for an interesting business book.

What I found, however, was a lot of books about "being at the top." In the world of business books, everyone apparently wants to be CEO of a company. All of the books I saw were about leading and being in charge.

But the fact is most of us are never going to be the CEO of anything. Moreover, many of us do not want to be. *What we do want is to survive middle and senior management, contribute to our companies as best we can, and get promoted every now and then.* We want to move up without struggling or being ineffectual.

That is when I realized how little support there is for middle managers. Even though middle managers are arguably the lifeblood of any corporation — and the butt of lots of jokes — *there is relatively little information available on how to do a good job as a middle manager, how to rise in the middle ranks, and how to handle the day-to-day challenges that make up most middle managers' jobs.*

Even within your own company, you are unlikely to find much help. Sure, the IBMs and GEs of the world provide great training. But what if you do not work for one of those companies? Where can you get advice about how to handle the everyday issues and challenges middle managers face? It is time to get unstuck and break away from the pack. It is time to find out how to be an effective 21st Century Executive.

To fill this void, I launched my website, the *3 Minute Mentor* (www.the3minutementor.com), and began posting a weekly video series. In each video, I discuss how to manage or deal with one specific issue or challenge. Each episode covers anything, from finding a mentor to dealing with an undermining team member.

To develop the content, I drew on my twenty-five-years-plus in corporate management. I began as a frontline customer support representative, plodded and struggled along, and moved all the way up to chief marketing officer for multiple Fortune 500 technology companies. I simply based each episode of the *3 Minute Mentor* on things I wish I had known at specific points in my career and the tools I developed on my own to succeed as a manager.

The response to the *3 Minute Mentor* has been overwhelming — and incredibly positive. I have heard from friends and managers working in companies of all sizes throughout the world. A police department in Australia is using the *3 Minute Mentor* material as part of its management training. The messages are variations of the same theme: "Thank you for helping me to solve a problem that had been keeping me awake at night. In other words, now I do less struggling and more managing."

My viewers have also been asking for more. They are eager for more insight into how to handle the day-to-day issues and challenges most managers face. It is easy to see why: *Most management training and development courses do not focus on those issues.* Mentors can be invaluable sources of support, but they may not be readily available to help deal with daily questions and situations. Even if you can go to or have been through a training course, the material you come away with is not always close by and easy to use.

One of the design principles for the *3 Minute Mentor* was that it had to be a resource "for the digital age." It had to be online, it had to be short, and it had to be easy to use. Over the first year, that has worked well. Subscribers seemed to respond to that design.

As the *3 Minute Mentor* expanded to include more than fifty episodes, people began asking for a better search capability so that they could more easily find and rewatch old episodes.

Eventually, even upgrading our search capability to index episodes on key subjects like management or leadership was not enough.

As the *3 Minute Mentor* approached its seventy-fifth episode, people wanted even better access to all of our content, and they wanted to be able to gift it to a colleague. Even in this digital age, people still make room for "hard copy" or at least a compendium of episodes. To that end, we created this book. The followers of the *3 Minute Mentor* now have something physical they can dip into and out of, and share with friends and colleagues.

IF YOU ASK A THOUSAND PEOPLE

As a marketing person, I am always looking for data, and I thought drawing on some data would benefit the book I was creating. To help with this, I created an At Work survey that more than one thousand people took online. The survey explored some of the issues, questions, and challenges relevant to avoid becoming a Stuck-in-the-Middle Manager in order to be an effective 21st Century Executive. What was striking was the way that people in the survey viewed and compared themselves to others.

The simplest example was around honesty, integrity, and trust, the subject of Chapter 7 of this book. When the survey asked the respondents if they act with honesty, integrity, and trust, not surprisingly, 98 percent said they do. When asked if other people act with honesty, integrity, and trust, 28 percent of the respondents said no. *Is some percentage of the 98 percent lying about their level of honesty, integrity, and trust?* No, they are not. This response simply points to one of the key ways to use this book. While some of the 98 percent were probably lying or at least deceiving themselves, this gap does not represent dishonesty but poor communication.

Having skills is of no use if you do not demonstrate those skills through your actions. It is not enough to *think of yourself as having* honesty, integrity, and trust. You need to *demonstrate* those qualities.

Knowing how to manage a project is all well and good, but that is of no use to anyone, including you, if people do not observe your ability to manage a project. Without that ability, you do not get credit for that skill.

To be a successful 21st Century Executive and thereby avoid the fate of a Stuck-in-the-Middle Manager, you cannot ineffectively communicate your knowledge or skills in your career or your job. You are competing with people who are actively managing their careers and demonstrating knowledge and skills every day. *You need to do the same.*

How to Use This Book

One of the common themes you will find in *Become a 21st Century Executive: Breaking Away from the Pack* is that there are few yes-or-no answers or black-and-white situations in management or when building a career. The most effective twenty-first century managers are *those who can evaluate available information and their options to make the best possible decision.* This book is designed to help you do that.

Each chapter focuses on one specific issue. Each chapter is a simple framework that you can use to analyze your unique situation and its potential variables to develop your own solution. These frameworks are there to help you make better decisions. Often, the chapters will have simple case studies of situations that I have seen over the years.

Above all, *Become a 21st Century Executive: Breaking Away from the Pack* is about making the right career choices. Most managers build their careers on a series of choices and an accumulation of knowledge and experience. A strong career requires making a series of good choices and having a plan.

Realize, too, a management career is a marathon, not a sprint. A wrong turn can take you off course and delay your development considerably — but it does not necessarily end the race.

What I do not provide is answers. I cannot tell you how to solve your problems *because no one single answer will work in every situation.*

There are no easy answers. Anyone who tells you otherwise is not telling the truth.

I want you to use this book to come up with your own answers:

- When you are interviewing job candidates for the first time;
- When you are having problems getting your boss to listen to you;
- When you are about to give or receive a difficult performance review;
- When you think things through before you resign from a job;
- When you are dealing with a significant change in your job or role.

Become a 21st Century Executive: Breaking Away from the Pack provides insight and guidance for these situations. More than that, you can read and digest each chapter in just a few minutes.

This book and its suggestions may not work for everyone or be appropriate for every situation. You can use this information when you have just a few minutes free and when the only other alternative would be going into a situation cold.

YOU ALWAYS REMEMBER GOOD ADVICE

I always remember the first piece of advice I got in my career: *the sooner you can admit that you have made a mistake, the easier it is to fix.* That was an important lesson for me at work. While it might seem obvious, learning it then taught me something else too: *the best advice is often the advice you can use quickly and easily.*

Become a 21st Century Executive: Breaking Away from the Pack and its companion website, the *3 Minute Mentor,* are here and available to give you advice when you need it. When you have a situation that is new to you and you are not sure how to handle it, let these resources help walk you through your options.

Visit the companion website for this book:
www.the3minutementor.com

SECTION I

MANAGING YOUR CAREER

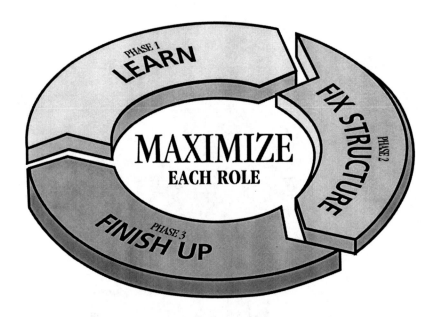

See more about Maximizing Each Role in Chapter 8.

ONE

Planning a Career

—⟨⟩—

*"Would you tell me, please, which way I ought to go
from here?"*
*"That depends a good deal on where you want to get to,"
said the Cat.*
"I don't much care where —" said Alice.
"Then it doesn't matter which way you go," said the Cat.
*"— so long as I get SOMEWHERE," Alice added as an
explanation.*
*"Oh, you're sure to do that," said the Cat, "if you only walk
long enough."*
Alice's Adventures in Wonderland

Unlike Alice, I have had a pretty good idea during my twenty-
five-year career of what I wanted to accomplish and where I
wanted to end up. Certainly, I have taken detours and done
things that I had not considered early on. However, the basic
trajectory went pretty much as I had planned. I attribute that to
always having the end goal in sight.

But not everyone does this. In early 2012, I conducted a survey
of more than one thousand professionals. The survey focused
on where people were in their career compared to where they
thought they would be. The results are interesting: only 18
percent of the respondents felt that they were ahead of where
they wanted to be; 38 percent indicated that they were behind

where they thought they would be; and approximately one in ten had never considered the question.

A key professional challenge is knowing how to plan a career. Without a career plan, it is easy to become stuck in the middle.

When I began my own career, I identified the major milestones for my career and roughly when I wanted to retire. In order to make sure I was heading in the right direction, I needed to know my final destination. I needed to decide whether those milestones and directions would be driven by money, some overarching goal like starting my own business, or achieving certain levels in a corporate environment.

In the end, I decided to pursue a career in marketing by working in large high-technology firms. I set an overall goal of being a chief marketing officer by the time I retired. For that to happen, I needed interim goals and a timeframe for achieving them. For example, by age twenty-five, I needed to be a manager of some sort. By age thirty-five, I wanted to rise to the senior director level. And so on.

When setting these goals, I wanted to make sure that (1) they would help me achieve my overall aspiration of becoming a chief marketing officer, and (2) that the goals were realistic and achievable within the stated timeframe. It was important not to set myself up for failure or frustration by having goals that I could not realistically achieve.

Having a plan in place, at least in my own mind, allowed me to focus my career decisions on moves that would help me accumulate and build the skills and experience necessary to move to the next level and closer to my ultimate goal of becoming chief marketing officer. This plan also helped me to understand the types of contacts and network I would need in order to achieve this goal.

No matter what your ultimate career goal is or how definitive that goal may be, it is worth taking the time to create a plan to achieve it. Without a plan, you will find it difficult to know if you are going in the right direction or staying on course. Without a timeline, even if you need to expand or contract it at different points, you will not have a realistic chance to achieve your objectives.

FOCUS ON THREE KEY QUESTIONS

The hardest thing about any career planning process is articulating where you want to end up. It is also the most important thing to do, *because stating the end goal will drive you through that process.* Effective career planning focuses on answering three key questions:

1. **Where do you want to go?**
2. **Where are you today?**
3. **How quickly do you want to get from here to there?**

Answering these questions may seem difficult, but doing so is essential to effective career planning.

1. Where do you want to go? It is never too early in your career to consider this question. You need to decide what success will look like for you at the end of your career. You need to articulate what matters to you and where you want to end up.

The answer to this question can certainly change over time, but it is the starting point for any career plan. Depending on what you ultimately want to achieve, this goal could be money, career status, social position, or anything else that could drive you to be successful.

Remember, this is about what *you* want, not what others expect from you. Your goal can help you define what is important to you, and where you think you are going to be when you retire.

2. Where are you today? Once you have articulated where you want to go in your career, it is time to assess where you are today relative to that goal. To determine where you are today, you can use the same process that you used to determine where you want to go.

If your goal focuses on money, take the time to review your current financial situation and determine where you are today moneywise compared to where you want to be. If your goal focuses on career position, define your current role, including your responsibilities and experience.

Where you are today is your starting point. Be honest about where that is, because it will help you determine the best way to achieve your ultimate goal.

3. How quickly do you want to get from here to there? The final step in this career planning process is drawing the line that will connect where you are today with where you are headed. How will you get from here to there?

To make this process easier, divide your timeframe into manageable chunks. If you want to own your own business or become a senior executive of a company in twenty years, divide that twenty years into smaller time frames of four or five years each. Do not make these intervals too short, or you may be setting yourself up for repeated failure. It is better to overachieve some steps by going faster than anticipated than to miss all of them because you did not give yourself enough time to achieve each level.

What can you do in the next five years to move yourself closer to your goal? If you want to become a chief financial officer within twenty years, you will need to take on a series of positions with progressively more responsibility within finance. In the current business climate, it also helps to gain experience in other areas of company operations. *What is the next role or position that you should attain on your journey?*

Take time to think about the steps you will need to take and how they fit in your chosen timeframe. Consider how you will move from your current position to, say, a director, and then on to vice president and so on.

Seek out and nurture strong relationships with mentors. This will be an important part of the process. A good mentor can help you identify gaps in your skills and guide you in developing a plan to address and close those gaps. See Chapter 11 for more on finding the right mentor.

For example, if you are currently a manager, you may need more advanced skills in engineering, finance, or some other area in order to be promoted to director. Because you are unlikely to move from one role to the next in one leap, you should plan your career moves to focus on positions where you can gain the needed knowledge and experience to help you advance.

Career progression usually requires a lateral move or two. Time spent in those lateral positions is likely to help you in the longer term. The key is to make sure every move you make adds something—skills, experience, knowledge, content, network—to help you succeed at the next level and move closer to your ultimate goal.

THE BOTTOM LINE

» Without a plan, you don't know if you are going in the right direction or staying on course.

NEXT STEPS

1. *End it:* write down where you want to be when you retire, and when you expect it to occur. Include whatever means the most to you—your net worth, your level, your location, or whatever else is important.

2. Backtrack: assess where you are now and what skills and experiences you will need to meet your retirement level and date.

3. *Plot it:* take steps in five-year increments to get you from where you are today to where you want to be.

4. *Talk* about *it:* show your partner, a close friend, or a relative your plan. See if this significant person in your life can offer further suggestion on how best to achieve your goal.

5. *Take it:* make the first step towards your goal.

TWO

JUDGING TALENT AND OPPORTUNITY

One of the most frustrating elements for people who get stuck in the middle of the pack at work is the lack of guidance they receive on the best way to evaluate talent and opportunity — their own, and that of others.

If you know how to judge talent and opportunity, you can make better decisions about your own career. You can also provide more and better performance and development discussions to your people by going beyond whether or not someone achieved his or her objectives.

People want feedback about how they are doing their jobs and how they are performing on their current projects and tasks. They want a sounding board for evaluating and making career decisions. They want advice on how to move up to a specific role. In this age of 360-degree feedback, people may need help in reviewing the performance of more senior people, their peers, and their subordinates.

In my own management experience, I have found that many HR- developed performance review and management systems do not support this type of in-depth coaching. Although there are many HR tools and processes that tell you what to do, there is little information about how to do it. The end result is that these tools tend to focus solely on whether people achieve their objectives and not how they have done so.

Good coaching and development focus on how individuals achieve their objectives and how they use what they know in doing so. Most traditional performance review and management tools do not provide simple models to help you look at those issues.

A MODEL FOR JUDGING TALENT AND OPPORTUNITY

To address this gap and to help you overcome these issues, I developed a model for judging talent. I generated this model during my first role as a director for a major corporation.

Almost as soon as I settled into my office, one of my team members told me that he wanted to move to a team he had worked on previously in order to take on the role of team leader. In this company, a team leader directs the work of the team but does not manage the people on the team. This team member expected this move to position him to become a manager more quickly than he would if he stayed on my team.

Unfortunately, his expectations were too optimistic. The move had the opposite effect. The team member's new role did not offer any opportunities to develop new and better content in the form of knowledge, skills, habits, understanding, or even an expanded network. Quite simply, he was taking on a job he had already done. As a result, his rise to manager, although it did happen eventually, was delayed considerably.

To help others avoid this type of result, my model focuses on three elements that go into developing a career: content, approach, and network. If my colleague had access to this model, I believe he would have been able to evaluate the team leader move more clearly and may have made a better decision instead of choosing a role where he got stuck quite some time. Instead, he went back to a job where he was not able to build his content knowledge, learn new skills and approaches, or

20

expand his network. He was thinking too short-term, and he was not evaluating his whole career.

You can use this model to *stop struggling and making improper choices* when making your own career decisions, evaluating potential hires, and organizing reviews and performance discussions. I continued using this process throughout my career to help myself and others identify new ways to contribute and develop. Each element is discussed in more detail in its own chapter as noted below.

1. Content. *Content* focuses on what the person brings to the workplace — knowledge, skills, and understanding. Many people get jobs and opportunities because of their specific knowledge, information, and context, not because they understand processes.

Until the last few years, career advice led people to develop content that focused too much on processes rather than adding value to a team and a company. When someone hires you, he or she is hiring your cumulative knowledge and talents. Therefore, when you evaluate career decisions and opportunities, *focus on what level and type of content these opportunities allow you to develop.*

If you are doing the hiring, you need to evaluate each candidate's content: *what content does each one need to have for the role?* When you are coaching someone, the focus will be on what additional content that person should add to the portfolio to increase his or her value and improve marketability.

See Chapter 3 for more details on Content.

2. Approach. *Approach* focuses on your ability to use what you know. It does not matter how smart you are if you are unable to use that knowledge effectively in a given role. That means being able to lead, delegate, drive a project to its next level, and display other capabilities necessary for success.

Approach should also factor into your choice for your next role. When you make a career move, make sure that the new role provides enough of an opportunity for you to put your knowledge into action and hone your approach.

When hiring someone, ask yourself, *What types of situations will this candidate encounter and need to manage?* If the candidate does not have the approach necessary to manage and deal with these situations, he or she would likely struggle and get stuck in the middle of the pack. When coaching someone, think about what that individual should be able to demonstrate in terms of leadership skills given his or her current level, as well as what he or she needs to add to reach more senior positions in the organization.

See Chapter 4 for more details on Approach.

3. Network. Your *network* is whom you know. A strong network is an essential tool when developing a career. You need to know people who can help you to move up and grow in your career, along with individuals who can help you to do your job well. If you know industry analysts, journalists, customers, and emerging talents, bring those resources to bear when doing your job. A strong network is an important safeguard against struggling and failing to lead because you can use that network to be effective in your job and to learn and grow.

Any employer or potential employer is as interested in your internal network within the company and your external network as it is in you. *Whom can you bring to the party? Whom can you influence?*

You need to build a strong network. And you need to know how to use that network effectively. Any new role should provide opportunities to develop and nurture your network.

When hiring someone, be sure to assess his or her internal and external networks. Consider what connections someone in that role will need. If you are coaching, ask your client to develop a picture of his or her network, including who is in it and who are the best and strongest connections. Using this visual, the individual can then build a plan to address missing links and strengthen weak bonds.

See Chapter 5 for more details on Network.

THE BOTTOM LINE

» Base your career growth and development on what you know (content), how you use what you know (approach), and whom you know (network).

NEXT STEPS

1. Objectively audit your content, approach, and network. Identify the critical gaps in each area, then set a three-step improvement plan into play.

2. Work on the three career growth elements as you move through your career. Use each of them to evaluate different opportunities, thereby improving your chances for professional success.

THREE

GET YOUR CONTENT CLEAR

The previous chapter focused on the three critical elements—content, approach, and network—so you can stop struggling in the midst of the pack and develop a successful career. Let's look more closely at content.

Content is the sum total of your knowledge, and your ability to use that knowledge to contribute to the company's decision-making capability. It is that "what you know" that gets you invited to the head table.

Your content needs to be both broad and deep, and it should not be limited to processes or applications. Here's why: *being an expert on specific processes simply is not very useful or compelling unless you are reengineering that process.* Content that focuses on processes alone is the hallmark of people who are at risk of becoming Stuck-in-the-Middle Managers.

By contrast, *content based on knowledge of procurement, sales, engineering, operations, and other parts of a business allows you real opportunities to guide your company in making better business decisions.* That increases the company's chances of success and can help reduce the costs or "bottom line." Knowledge of your products, the markets in which you operate, and the customers who buy your products, can be even more valuable. With this knowledge, you can make a more significant contribution both to your company and its "top line" profit. Most businesses are

24

looking for growth, and give greater rewards to people who build the "top line."

BUILDING LEVELS OF CONTENT

There is more than one way to build content. Let's take the case of two managers, George and Phil, both of whom were trying to expand their content but were taking two different approaches.

With existing expertise in sales support, George wanted to develop new content by moving into a role in customer service. George's rationale for this choice was that the requirements for the customer service role were similar enough to skills needed in sales to give him a foothold in the area and an understanding of the new position so that he was not starting out "cold." At the same time, the role was different enough to allow him to develop and expand his content significantly.

George's approach was a sound one, and within two years, he had moved up to become a director on the sales team based largely on the content he had developed using this approach. While this approach was an easy way to accelerate his career in the short- to mid-term, George still needed to move to different departments within the company to round out his content.

By contrast, Phil, whose experience was in quality assurance, opted for a role in Human Resources that was completely different and unconnected to his current work. Phil's choice reflected his desire to expand his content base rapidly by taking on new roles as often as possible throughout his company.

This approach slowed down Phil's career progression. Rather than helping him to build his content, Phil's move to HR was a tactical mistake. He was so unfamiliar with the work and requirements that he spent much of his first months just learning the basics and the processes. As a result, Phil was unable to quickly add to his content knowledge. However, Phil's tenure in HR was likely to prove beneficial for building his long-term career.

When choosing the best way to build content in your own career path, remember that careers last *decades*, not years or months. In the long run, both George and Phil were smart to add new content into their portfolios. Although both men may end their careers at similar levels (in the short term), George's move was more tactical while Phil's was more strategic.

As these examples show, acquiring and developing content is a bit like playing a video game. At each level, you pick up new skills, but you also leverage what you have previously learned. If you move up too fast without gaining the knowledge you need in order to be effective and succeed, your tenure on the fast track could be very short-lived.

Consider carefully the type of content you want or need to develop for your content portfolio. Are you going to be a specialist with deep knowledge in a specific area, or more of a general manager who maintains a broader view of operations? How you answer this question will drive your thinking and decisions about content development.

Let's say you want to be the world's greatest expert when it comes to a piece of equipment like *wheels*. Wheel specialists possess expert and detailed knowledge of what the wheel does. So you need to know how wheels are made and what goes wrong when they are made badly. You probably need to know the history of the wheels, and even own a few patents on steps to produce better ones. On the other hand, if you want to be a general manager in the plant that produces wheels, all this specific knowledge, while interesting, is not *required*. In the case of the general manager, becoming too knowledgeable or too detailed in one particular area is not going to help you succeed in that role. You need knowledge that is broader but not necessarily as deep or detailed in a lot of areas.

Your content needs change as you move through the organization. You build your content portfolio to meet those needs. For example, to avoid getting stuck when you are managing a small group of people who are all working on similar content, you need to know as much, if not more, about the team's content as your team members. As you move up to more senior management positions, your content needs to become both broader and deeper. As the CMO of a technology company, I routinely relied on my twenty-five years of experience to talk about the history and evolution of the technology industry, as well as its future direction.

How to Build Content

You develop content in three ways: through academics, on the job and via life experience. Traditionally, at the beginning of your career, you learn content and, if all goes well, you are teaching content at your career's end. The smart 21st Century Executive knows that you never stop learning.

SCHOOLING FOR CONTENT

An obvious way to develop content while acquiring knowledge is by leveraging training and formal education to earn an undergraduate or graduate degree or certification in a specific area.

Pursuing an advanced degree, like an MBA, can help you hone your modeling and analytical skills. Recognize that the degree alone may not be sufficient to help you expand your content significantly. Some of the content you gain through studying for such degrees is likely to be theoretical. Getting stuck and being ineffective occurs when you have difficulty translating theories into real-life decision-making.

Still, a degree does provide a new baseline of knowledge that you can leverage in a new role. With this type of grounding, you can take a much faster path while learning on the job.

ON-THE-JOB CONTENT

I have found that the best way to develop content is by *doing something*. What you know is generally a result of what you have done—i.e., taking on more challenging jobs and roles in different divisions and companies, and even living in different countries.

As George's experience shows, one of the best ways to develop your content is to build it gradually by moving to adjacent areas that allow you to develop more and deeper content in a specific area. By moving into an adjacent content space, you are more likely to find that your existing content or knowledge overlaps somewhat with the new area. As a result, you can leverage that existing content to become effective in your new role more quickly.

As Phil learned, you may think that moving to a completely new area where you have little or no experience or knowledge is the fastest way to build your content. But that approach limits your productivity and often means you may get stuck in your new role. Instead of spending the first several months planning and implementing changes and pursuing improvement opportunities in the new role, you spend most of your time learning the ropes of the new area with little time for anything that will improve performance. As a result, you will neither develop much new content nor make much of a difference in your role.

LIFE-EXPERIENCE CONTENT

Gaining new content is not limited to the classroom or the office. Just living your life exposes you to new content. If you have lived abroad, served on nonprofit boards, or painted houses during college summers, all of those experiences add to your content. Being able to talk with and lead people from different backgrounds, cultures, and countries is a crucial skill in this global business environment. The ability to give presentations at conferences and to convince large groups of people of the value of your ideas is also important.

Here is one cautionary note regarding content. For most people, neither academics nor past experience alone is enough to ensure your continued progression to higher levels and new roles. I have known colleagues with twenty years of experience who have fallen prey to Stuck-in-the-Middle Management because they did not keep their content current. These people wonder why their careers stalled. I have also met many newly minted MBAs in their twenties who wonder why they are not yet running the company.

No matter what kind of degree or experience you have, you are always going to compete with others who also have a lot to offer. Those individuals may have more content, better approaches and stronger networks. *It is up to you to manage your own content development in order to stand out.*

THE BOTTOM LINE

» You can get invited to the "head table" by gaining and delivering knowledge both broad and deep.

NEXT STEPS

1. Ask your colleagues to identify the content for which you are best known. *What would others say you are an expert in?*

2. On your own, outline some key areas of content *weakness* in your content portfolio. Then, sign up for a course or training in one such area.

3. Commit to learning *one new area of content each year,* whether it's through a course or via at-home research.

FOUR

GET KNOWN FOR YOUR APPROACH

Chapter 2 focused on the three critical elements — content, approach, and network — that help you avoid Stuck-in-the-Middle Management while developing a successful career. Let's look more closely at *approach*.

If content is "what you know," then approach is "using what you know." As such, it is an important element of career success. The roots of an organization plagued by Stuck-in-the-Middle Managers can often be traced to managers and executives who have a weak approach.

To understand why, consider what a strong approach can do for you and your colleagues. *A strong approach allows you to work well with others, to share your knowledge freely, and to apply that knowledge to help your team accomplish its goals.* With a strong approach, you can find ways to help the people around you to perform at their best and to grow in their work.

All of us know people with whom no one wants to work. Sometimes, these are brilliant people who do not "play well with others." Sometimes, these individuals just want to sit in the corner and do the work themselves. In other cases, these people talk a big game but do very little and accomplish even less. If these types of people do not strengthen their approach, they are likely to become Stuck-in-the-Middle Managers who will stall in their careers eventually.

You do not have to be at one of these extremes to find that a poor approach is hurting your career. Whenever I talk to people about their work and their career prospects, I help them identify weaknesses in their approach that could be holding them back.

Stella was an up-and-coming team leader who I expected to move steadily upward toward management and above. However, Stella needed to work on some areas of her approach. First, she needed to improve her problem-solving skills. Stella had excellent content in her area of operations. She got bogged down when her team members hit a roadblock and needed her help to solve the underlying problem. Second, Stella had little experience in presenting her ideas to others and in gaining their support for those ideas. I traced this particular weakness to a lack of practice and opportunity rather than to any personal shortcoming. I advised Stella to actively seek out opportunities to make presentations to more senior people inside and outside of the company to gain more experience in that area.

Stella could build her approach by getting a mentor. (We talk more about that in Chapter 11.) Few good courses or books exist on how you can improve your approach, but if you isolate the area or topic you want to work on and search for it online, you may find the help you need. For example, the *3 Minute Mentor* site is updated regularly, and you can find lots of content there beyond what is included in this book.

STRENGTHENING YOUR APPROACH

To strengthen your approach, focus on three basic elements: how you work, how you work with others, and how you lead.

If you do not know how well you perform on each element, or if you suspect that you need to work on something in particular, ask a peer, manager, or mentor for feedback and advice.

HOW YOU WORK

Working on autopilot is a hallmark of a stalled, Stuck-in-the-Middle Manager. To strengthen your approach, consider how you get your work done:

- Are you able to get started on something on your own, or do you need someone to explain every task?
- Do you analyze and solve problems using data, and do you provide insights based on something more concrete than your own opinion?
- Can you present your ideas in a logical and compelling way?
- Do you provide work that people can use immediately, or does the work require a lot of reworking on others' part?

It is important to realize that most of what you do at work has been done by someone else many times before. Someone on your team or in your organization has worked a similar problem, goal, or deliverable. To leverage that capability, I try to identify the things that my friends and colleagues are good at and learn from them. As a manager, I help my team members strengthen the parts of their overall approach where they do not currently excel by pairing them with someone who does excel at that approach. The more you help yourself and others to strengthen their approach proactively, the better off you, your colleagues, and the team as a whole will be.

Another element of approach is how well you present your ideas and plans. Unlike calculus at school, a successful approach does not require that you show how you got to the answer. You must always consider to whom you are presenting when you determine how and what to present. It is important to remember that a bad presentation can overpower the quality of the work. See Chapter 14 for more on how to make your presentations more effective.

How You Work with Others

Working well with others is a crucial part of your approach. Consider the following questions when evaluating your strength in this area:

- Can you escalate and resolve a problem or situation successfully without unnecessary conflict?
- Do you always have to lead, or can you play a secondary role when necessary?
- In difficult situations, are you able to reach out to others and form alliances?

Few jobs exist in the modern world that do not require working with other people. Of all the elements of approach, working well with others can be the skill with the potential either to accelerate your career the most—or to quickly steer it toward Stuck-in-the-Middle Management.

You need to work well with others whether you like it or not, and even when you think you could do the work faster without the rest of the team. Others will judge you harshly if you do not develop this part of your approach.

Inevitably, you will encounter someone with whom you just cannot work for whatever reason. Sometimes, the reasons are understandable and logical, and sometimes the reasons are beyond understanding. Whatever the specifics of the situation, it is important that you deal with it and do not ignore it.

When I was a junior salesman for a large insurance company in the UK, the key buyer on one account didn't like me for some reason. I still do not know what I said or did to offend him, but it was clear he wasn't going to buy anything from me. Although it had the potential to make me look bad, I realized I had to tell my boss about the situation.

This turned out to be the best approach to the problem. Rather than reflecting badly on me, my boss understood that I was trying to do what was best for the company and he reassigned the customer to a different sales representative. In this case, my responsibility was to the company and not to my ego. Any bruising my ego took in the short term was mitigated when my manager told me that my action was very "mature."

How You Lead

Working as a leader requires a completely different skill set than you need to be part of a team. Ineffective management occurs when people do not know how to lead.

When evaluating your leadership skills, consider the following questions:

- Can you bring a team together and drive team members to work faster than they want?
- Do you deliver work and results on time?
- Do you know when and how to escalate a situation, and how to deal appropriately with a situation that someone else has escalated?
- At the end of a project, does your team feel like everyone shared the credit and success of a job well done?

We talk about the difference between leadership and management in Chapter 25. What we are discussing here is *not* management. It is not even about using your organizational power to get things done. In your career, you will be judged on how well you work as part of a team in order to help that team complete the task at hand. This is the case whether or not you are the leader of the team.

Part of honing your approach is learning the models and techniques used to move a group meeting forward. In group sessions, I prefer to lead with the flip-chart pen in my hand. I do this not because I know more or want to control the conversation; rather, I do this to help the team achieve a greater work output by helping to structure the conversation. While this example does not involve managing the team or running the meeting, it is still an example of leadership.

THE BOTTOM LINE

» A poor approach hurts your career, but a strong approach gets the job done — and done well.

NEXT STEPS

1. Consider three people who work effectively and outline the skills and approaches you think they have and use. Then assess your own skills and approaches in light of theirs.

2. Ask one of those individuals to mentor you for two months' time. When that time interval is up, assess your progress. Determine if you need further coaching and who is best to teach you.

FIVE

BUILDING THE RIGHT NETWORK

—◄◄◖◗▸▸—

Chapter 2 focused on the three critical elements — content, approach, and network — that help you avoid a career stall while simultaneously positioning yourself for success. Let's look more closely at building a *network*.

In Chapters 3 and 4, we talked about what you know (content) and how you use what you know (approach). The old adage that "Building a career is not about what you know, but whom you know" still holds some truth. The third element in building a career that can help you avoid Stuck-in-the-Middle Management is your network of people inside and outside your company.

In many ways, your network resembles the ripples that form when you throw a stone into a pond. The core of that ripple represents the people with whom you work right now and whom you know well. As the ripples spread out, they extend to the members of your broader team: people working in other departments and divisions of your company; people working in other companies within your industry; and people working outside of the industry.

The broader and more extensive your network, the better positioned you are. I have been involved in talent evaluations in which the group conducting the evaluations did not consider someone seriously for a new role or promotion because some members of the group did not know that person. If the key decision makers in your company do not know you, they cannot fairly evaluate your potential. That lack of network is seen as the candidate's fault.

A strong network is a fundamental tool for building a career; do not limit your network to your employer's phone directory. Put equal effort into establishing and building the network outside your company. A weak network not only can lead to a career stall, but also can reflect poorly on your ability to influence a broader community, including people within your industry, the press, customers, analysts, and others.

Build a strong network, and you can leverage it to keep from becoming stuck in the middle and do your job better. Use your network to find a mentor, to become a mentor, to get a promotion, to raise money for a good cause, or to do any number of other things to further your career.

BUILDING A NETWORK

Networking does not have to be some organized event where everyone swaps business cards and makes small talk. Every day at work, we meet new people and exchange information and business cards. This is the simplest and most obvious form of networking, and it shows that *networking should be a part of every day*. Every person you meet at work and through your family, friends, and acquaintances can become part of your network.

Although there can be overlap between your personal network and your work network, we will focus on the network in your career.

The first thing you need to remember about building a network is that it should reach beyond the people you work with each day and the people in your company as a whole. A vibrant network includes customers, partners, suppliers, and even people you meet at trade shows. Every interaction you have with these individuals is key to growing your network.

Next, as you meet potential members for your network, help them get a sense of who you are, what you do, and where you are going with your career. Try to get this same information from the other person. You initiate this type of conversation by saying, "If ever there is anything I can do...." That is usually enough to find common ground in what you both can do for each other.

If you exchange business cards with someone, don't just throw the card in your desk drawer. Write on the back of the card what was interesting or important about that person. Pull out the card to refresh your memory if you ever need to communicate with that person at a later date. After all, you never know when you are going to meet someone again. I recall being ignored by people who knew me in order for them to speak to someone else in the room they deemed more important. I learned from that and try to make each connection with people at work memorable.

A few years ago, I met with a consultant who was writing a report on my company. By luck, I remembered him and how we had met more than ten years earlier when I was working for another company. That previous meeting had not gone well for me. He had metaphorically "beaten me up" for an hour. The good news is that experience provided an important perspective to the current meeting. I used it as a way to make a joke while also crediting him with his insight and guidance during the meeting. The consultant remembered the meeting and was happy with the way I recounted it. That meeting led to a friendship that lasts to this day, and I value his guidance. You never know when people might come back into your life.

When you think about becoming a 21st Century Executive, you have to think about the 21st Century tools you have to support your efforts. In today's digital age, we have great tools for maintaining our networks like LinkedIn, Facebook, and Twitter. Not only are these tools useful to broaden our networks, they allow us to have conversations daily with influencers, and enable us to get and give advice to our networks constantly. It is worth remembering that these tools, while they appear to be private, can suddenly become very public. Never write or say something on a social media site or tool that you wouldn't want out in public.

One piece of advice about Facebook that I really like came from someone who would remind people that it was a tool designed for family and friends, not colleagues. I follow that rule, and only "friend" people I know well. If I receive "friend" requests from people in my work life on Facebook, I suggest that they invite me to link with them on LinkedIn, or follow me on Twitter.

USING A NETWORK

The care and feeding of your network is very important. The members of your network are like friends: *abuse them and you will lose them.* If you keep asking for favors and information without providing anything in return, you will alienate your network. People may still like you, but they are unlikely to go out of their way to help you.

Do things for people without expecting anything in return, and don't ask someone to do something for you unless you offer to return the favor—*and mean it.* If you offer to help someone in a specific way, you need to be in a position to make good on that offer. Often when I am meeting with someone, I will end the meeting by asking, "And is there anything else I can do for you?" This doesn't always get a response or request, but people will remember that you asked the question. If you do get an answer, it can often lead to information that you might not have gotten out of them during the meeting.

You do need to be cautious about referencing. If someone asks you for a reference, carefully consider the request and try to fulfill it. If you choose to do so, you don't have to do anything but tell the truth. Just keep in mind that when you are important to someone's network, one day that person could be important in your network.

To manage a network more easily, consider dividing it into three parts:

1. A **reference network** will help you get a new job. Remember to offer to be a job reference for others whenever you can. They need the help, too.
2. A **promotion network** should be made up of as many of the senior people in your company as possible. This can help ensure that you are considered for any new role or promotion that fits your profile.
3. An **objective network** helps you to do your work and achieve your objectives. Everyone needs help with work every now and then. A good objective network offers a great source of advice and guidance whenever you need information and favors to get something done on the job, and to avoid struggling and stalling on your career path.

MAINTAINING A NETWORK

Maintaining a network takes time and effort. This time and effort is well worth it, as it is a critical investment in your future. Without a strong network, it is difficult to achieve your objectives and makes it easier to get caught up in Stuck-in-the-Middle Managing.

Be prepared to put into your network as much as you take out by:

1. Acting as a reference;
2. Offering support and sharing experiences when people need help;
3. Volunteering to be on projects that are important to key members of your network;
4. Sharing resumes and job opportunities.

If the love you get is equal to the love you give (see the Beatles), then the value you get out of your network will be at least equal to the amount of effort you put into it. Try hard every day to add value to your network and the people in it. Go out of your way to extend the courtesy and support you might want if you were in another's shoes. My experience is that if you are there for the members of your network when they need you, those people will be there for you when you need them.

The Bottom Line

» Your network is more about *who knows you* than *whom you know.*

Next Steps

1. If you don't have a LinkedIn profile, create one.

2. For your *reference* network: once your LinkedIn profile is complete, send out LinkedIn invites to five colleagues (both former and present is fine) each week for the next four weeks.

3. For your *promotion* network: figure out which senior people already "have your back," then commit to adding at least one person to this group each year. Do so by volunteering on projects that are important to this particular individual.

4. For your *objective* network: ask a member of your team for help the next time you are stuck on a project.

SIX

HUNGER AND PRESENCE: DEVELOPING INTANGIBLES

What if you feel that you are doing everything right and are well positioned to move into the executive ranks, but you keep getting overlooked? Two important but intangible elements can help you get ahead — and become a 21st Century Executive.

When people tell me that their careers are stalled, I evaluate them on two key intangibles: hunger and presence.

Discussing hunger and presence is difficult. Unlike content, approach, and network, hunger and presence tend to be assessed primarily on qualitative (rather than quantitative) terms. Intangibles are, by their nature, a matter of opinion. Some people struggle with the idea of being assessed on intangibles, because these assessments are easily swayed by personal biases. *Yet, as you climb the corporate ladder, the reality is that you will be increasingly judged on things that boil down to people's opinions.* Your choice is whether you want to work to ensure that those opinions are positive.

HUNGER

Hunger is often confused with *ambition*. There is a big difference between the two.

Ambition drives you to seek promotion and power. Hunger is the willingness to do what is necessary to achieve your goals and ambitions.

It is not enough to say that you want to become an executive. You have to show that you are willing to do what it takes to achieve that goal. Here are some signs that you have the necessary hunger:

- You take jobs or assignments that others refuse;
- You are willing to do tasks because they are important, not because they are easy or will lead to attention and praise;
- You work longer hours than most;
- You tend to be around when someone needs an extra set of hands.

At one point in my career, I had to evaluate two finalists for promotion to a director position.

Grace was an up-and-coming manager with an MBA who talked a great deal about her desire to move up in her career. She had sought out the promotion by developing contacts with more senior people in the company, and she talked all the time about "being promoted."

The other candidate, Rachel, was just as ambitious. However, Rachel talked less about promotion and, instead, focused on getting more done, being responsive to her team and colleagues, building an impressive portfolio of results, and generally becoming the go-to person in her department.

Rachel clearly demonstrated more *hunger.* More importantly, she chose to demonstrate it in ways that would benefit her colleagues and the company. As candidates, both Grace and Rachel had similar content and approach and broad networks. Across those categories, both were pretty much equal.

Because the new role was for a director, I recognized that the position required more than just an experienced manager. A director needs to be hungry. Once I considered both candidates from that perspective, the choice for the director job was easy. I offered Rachel the job, and she accepted it.

Not surprisingly, Grace was not happy with my decision. She argued that it was her "turn" because she had been with the company and had been lobbying for the promotion longer. Unfortunately for Grace, she had been up against someone who had chosen to work harder and smarter in order to get ahead.

Grace's mistake was not her expressed intention to be promoted to an executive position. If you, as an employee, want to be considered for promotion opportunities, you need to let your boss know that. After all, if you don't think of yourself that way, why should they? Instead, Grace's mistake was not putting in the right kind of effort to achieve the results that would help her earn that promotion.

When people evaluate your hunger to succeed, they quickly see whether you have it. People see who pitches in, who works longer hours, who responds quickly to e-mails and phone calls, and so on—in short, who really wants more responsibility and advancement. Skill levels of two candidates being equal, I think most executives would choose the hungrier of the two for promotion.

Some employees, both junior and senior, balk at being measured on intangibles like hunger and presence. Many more junior employees are often uncomfortable being judged on criteria that are not clearly articulated. In modern society, everyone wants to know the rules and how they will be judged. With this thinking, it could be argued that it is not fair to give people a promotion or opportunity if they did something that wasn't "in the rules." There is, of course, some truth to this, so here's what you can do.

While it is difficult to incorporate "that extra bit" in basic job specifications, there are ways to signal the behavior you are looking for. In employees' annual review, you can indicate to employees when they have or have not "stretched themselves." You can also target awards to the individuals or teams in your group as a way to publicly recognize those who showed the type of initiative you want. Don't practice Stuck-in-the-Middle Management by always giving the top grade in these reviews to employees just for completing their work assignments. *You should expect your employees to "do more."*

When dealing with more senior employees, remember that not everyone wants to be an executive. In our At Work survey, about half of the respondents wanted to be an executive when they retired. Only 16 percent wanted to rise as far as the "C-level suite." Interestingly, nearly twice as many men than women (20 percent vs. 11 percent) believed they will be at that level one day.

The fact that not everyone aspires to the executive level is good news. After all, companies need more senior staff members who get the work done efficiently and effectively than they do future executives. These less hungry individuals will not express the same amount of hunger as more junior or ambitious employees, but they may be as or more essential to actually getting the work done. You need to be sure that you reward these individuals, too—but probably not with promotions.

PRESENCE

Most senior managers and executives have a certain *presence* or aura when they communicate verbally. This presence is a key reason for their being in senior positions.

When you address company employees, the board of directors, customers, shareholders and other important groups, what you say and how you say it matter quite a bit.

If you want to move up to a senior management or executive position, verbal skills are far more important than writing skills. To develop these verbal skills and presence:

- Develop your public speaking ability;
- Learn to communicate quickly and efficiently. Many senior executives only have a minute or two or even a few seconds to make their points and capture the attention of the people around them;
- Work on answering questions in a clear and compelling way;
- Be an engaged listener who quickly understands what people are saying and who asks questions that demonstrate that understanding.

Some people are born with this type of presence. The rest of us have to develop and nurture it. Practice, experience, and feedback are the keys to developing these skills. You can take courses, join Toastmasters, and accept speaking engagements as often as possible. At every point in your career, look for chances to present to customers and conferences, and identify other opportunities to speak.

As a manager, a significant area in which to coach your team is presentation skills and presence. Whenever someone presents at a big meeting or group session, make sure you give him or her feedback. This feedback needs to include what he or she did well and what he or she did poorly.

I worked once with a very senior executive who always made presentations using great charts that were full of strong content. Unfortunately, his presentation skills were limited to him reading the charts to the audience. He had learned this by not preparing or practicing before presenting to big meetings. Not only was this distracting to the audience, it minimized the important content in the presentation. To address this, I praised the quality of his work, but highlighted that his presentation style might be limiting its effectiveness. He had not even noticed that he was turning his back on the audience, and quickly corrected the behavior.

Finally, while it may not seem obvious, *listening* is an essential skill and part of presence. Being an engaged or active listener is a skill that you must learn and practice. Consider enrolling in a course on the subject. You will learn that listening is more than hearing: it is understanding, remembering, and using. More simply, you can just remember the lesson that someone once taught me: you have two ears and one mouth; use them in that proportion!

THE BOTTOM LINE

» As you climb the corporate ladder, you will be increasingly judged on things that boil down to people's opinions.

NEXT STEPS

1. Think about how you demonstrate professional hunger to your boss — and what your boss is likely to assume about your career intentions based on your actions.

2. Assess your own team to identify which team members are demonstrating hunger and a desire to move up. *What are you doing to foster and reward that behavior?*

3. Learn about, and then practice, engaged or active listening.

4. To develop your presence, sing up for a public speaking course.

5. The next time you speak at a meeting, deliver your main points in one or two minutes.

SEVEN

Do the Right Thing: Honesty, Integrity, and Transparency

In this Internet-enabled world, you need to conduct yourself the right way: with honesty, integrity, and transparency *at all times*. Too many people run into trouble every day by not following this advice. A lack of honesty, integrity, and transparency too often leads to your becoming a Stuck-in-the-Middle Manager.

You will inevitably meet and deal with colleagues and clients who "play games" or think they are more clever than everyone else. Even if you are intent on doing the right things, those good intentions can go awry when you deal with this type of person. *To keep from struggling in, and stalling, your career, never negotiate your core principles.*

Also, note that your decisions about honesty, integrity, and transparency in your personal life have consequences on how others think of you. One of my friends pointed out that people who have affairs at work often do not see how their colleagues perceive them. If someone is not honest with their spouse, you can assume they are generally not honest at all — and that means at work, too.

As we noted in the introduction, nearly all who responded to the At Work survey thought they act with honesty, integrity, and transparency. In fact, only 2 percent said they did not—and five people didn't even want to go there, and refused to answer the question! Curiously, although nearly everyone described themselves as honest, having integrity, and being transparent, they also believed that one in four of their colleagues was not.

Given that gap, let us look more closely at honesty, integrity, and transparency. Clearly, these traits are not as black-and-white as we may think.

HONESTY

Being honest in business might seem self-evident, but the business world is littered with failures rooted in common dishonesty. A company like Enron did not start out as a dishonest enterprise. Its problems began gradually, then slowly crept through its operations, with many otherwise decent people getting caught up in an increasingly dishonest environment.

The same thing can happen to you. A bad decision here, a bit of spin there, and maybe a little white lie thrown in for good measure—and suddenly you are operating in a dishonest way. You are lying to your colleagues, customers, suppliers, and, probably, yourself.

Let's say you work in a global company and one of your customers hints that a small payment to the right people can get things moving faster. You are under pressure to make the sale, and such payments are a "normal" part of doing business in that part of the world. The customer does not understand why you are reluctant to do what everyone else does in the course of business.

So what do you do? Pay the bribe, and you could be arrested under your country's anticorruption laws. Pay the bribe, and run afoul of legal regulations, like the Foreign Corrupt Practices Act of 1977 (if your employer is a publicly traded company). Don't pay the bribe—and you could lose the sale in a market in which your company is working diligently to gain a foothold.

Even if you pay the bribe and nothing happens, the transaction could be revealed years later in some unrelated audit or investigation. If that happens, the potential for lying and covering up opens up a host of other honesty-related questions.

Situations that test your commitment to honesty happen all of the time:

- You tell a customer something about a competitor that you know is either not true or based on unsubstantiated rumors;
- Someone sends you a document marked "Confidential" by mistake. You read it even though you know it was not intended for you and you are not authorized to do so. Consciously or not, what you read influences your future actions and decisions;
- At bonus time, you realize that your boss changes some paperwork to boost the department's results—and you say nothing about it.

Be dishonest in these situations—and the repercussions could follow you for the rest of your career.

Be honest even when it is not an easy thing to do, and you will be much better off in the long term.

INTEGRITY

Everything you say and do, combined with how you behave, reflects on your integrity. You either have integrity or you do not. *There is no middle ground.*

At one point, a former colleague of mine was working for, and drawing full-time paychecks from, two different companies. This person worked off-site and had a great deal of freedom in his movement and how he spent his time. In the end, he was found out because he was unable to meet the requirements of either employer.

Clearly, that individual lacked integrity. However, the people my colleague worked with had long suspected this individual and chose not to report him. Does that mean those people also lacked integrity? My answer is yes.

People with integrity do not remain quiet when they know someone is doing something wrong, when they know someone is not being treated equally, or when they know something inequitable is going on. Even worse is when someone compromises their own integrity to take action that allows the situation to continue even though they do not participate in the wrongdoing themselves.

Flagging when your colleague or your boss is being dishonest or showing lack of integrity is clearly a minefield that needs to be crossed carefully. Not only is it tough to do, but, if done poorly, it could cost you more than if you choose to look the other way. *Having integrity means you do the right thing regardless of the consequences.* Any time I have been in this situation, my first stop has been to a friend in Human Resources. This approach has two benefits. First, you get good advice on what to do next. Second, you register the issue with someone else. If you fear retaliation, it is good to get it on the record.

People who think they have no issues with integrity should consider how they manage their expense account. Handling expense money the same way you handle your own money is an example of integrity. Don't waste it to show off, and don't claim common expenses when you have not incurred them. It never fails to amaze how many people would risk the security of their high-paying job by cheating on their expenses to get a few extra dollars.

Having integrity means:

- Meeting your commitments;
- Behaving in accordance with your ethics;
- Treating people equally;
- Owning up to a mistake quickly, so it can be corrected.

Safeguard your integrity. Once you lose it, it is very difficult to get it back.

TRANSPARENCY

Transparency is all about sharing and not hiding information from others. If you think this is not important, think again. Lack of transparency is the lifeblood of the Stuck-in-the-Middle Manager, while full transparency is a key skill in a 21st Century Executive.

I remember a former colleague who would never reveal his thoughts or conclusions, or share any information, until the end of a conversation or meeting. His goal was to gain an advantage over everyone by keeping things to himself until it was in his best interest to reveal it. Once people realized this, they stopped trusting him and no longer included him in decision-making and discussions. His lack of transparency, and the other behaviors it bred, hurt his credibility and career significantly.

There are both positive and negative effects of transparency. *Negative transparency* occurs when you share information inappropriately. For example, if you are giving someone a bad performance rating or a low salary increase, negative transparency is providing information in order to place the blame for those unpleasant things on someone else, like your boss.

Positive transparency occurs when people share information (both good news and bad news) openly to aid decision-making and problem-solving. Positive types of transparency create an environment with few, or ideally no, secrets. A transparent business is much less likely to suffer from the effects of Stuck-in-the-Middle Managers because everyone will quickly know who is struggling or not taking ownership versus who adds value, leads, and learns. Running a business is not a poker game. Everyone should be committed to bringing out all relevant facts and decisions in order to do what is best for the business.

Sometimes, even the most senior people in a company are guilty of playing games with transparency by keeping things hidden that should be out in the open. Even if these senior people are not Stuck-in-the-Middle Managers, their behavior keeps others in the dark. As a result, these other individuals are more likely to get stuck and be inefficient because they do not have the information or insight to operate otherwise. In the long run, this damages a business.

THE BOTTOM LINE

» It is not always easy to act with honesty, integrity, and transparency—but if you don't, your actions are likely to backfire at some point.

NEXT STEPS

1. Consider the last difficult situation you were in and assess if you acted with honesty, integrity, and transparency. What could you have done differently?

2. Talk to your team about transparency. Ask them to highlight areas where they worry you are not being transparent with them.

3. Next time you think someone is not acting with honesty, integrity, or transparency, challenge them to be more open. Just be careful when and where you do so. Done in public, it might be viewed as an attack. This is much better done one-on-one.

EIGHT

WHEN TO FIND A NEW ROLE

When to move from one role to another is among the most important career decisions you will make. Career decisions call for a balance among the need to get the most out of each role and the need to continue developing and to avoid the appearance of stagnation. Stagnation can easily lead to struggling—and is something you want to avoid at all costs.

The key is to *know when it is time to stick with a role — and when it is time to move on.*

I remember working with two managers, Rachel and Harry, who were considered rising stars.

Rachel had a plan in place even before she worked a single day in a new role. She knew what she could get out of fulfilling that role, and probably how long it would take her to wring every bit of potential out of it.

She also understood that if she were to keep moving on and up, she needed to demonstrate that she had mastered her current role and was ready for the next big thing.

Harry, by contrast, was a creature of habit. Once he settled into a particular role, he got comfortable, then bogged down, in the day-to-day details of management. As a result, company executives soon considered Harry "essential" in that role. In fact, he became synonymous with it. Harry became both a practitioner and a victim of Stuck-in-the-Middle Management.

Harry's problem was that he never thought through what he could get out of the role from a career perspective, how long he should plan to be in that role, or how he could recognize when it was time to move on to something else. Unlike Rachel, he stayed in one role so long that eventually he was not considered a candidate for promotion because he was seen as irreplaceable in his current role. This is one of the worst outcomes for people who get caught up in a role: they stall out in what has become a "comfort zone" role for them.

MAXIMIZE EACH ROLE

As noted before, managing a career is like playing a video game. You want to move up to the next level as soon as you can. However, before you do so, you need to pick up new skills and capabilities that will help you to move on and survive at that next level.

Sometimes people want to move too quickly between roles, while others don't move quickly enough.

In my experience, each job or role has three phases. Once you have completed all three phases, you are likely to be ready to move up to the next level and take on another role. In most cases, managers should expect to spend about six months in each phase. If you are still in Phase One after eighteen months, you may be headed towards becoming a Stuck-in-the-Middle Manager. You need to rethink what you are doing and whether this role is right for your skills and capabilities if you want to become a 21st Century Executive.

Sometimes, if you are on the "fast track to the top," you can complete all the phases in much less than eighteen months. However, I have found that to be unusual, and it may indicate that you were either overqualified for the role to begin with, or your career is on a very fast track. Nearly two-thirds (63 percent) of the people in our At Work survey believed that you need to be in a role for at least two years, and more than half thought three years in a role is more appropriate. While many people may think that they want to be on the "fast track," fewer than one in five believe that less than eighteen months is a realistic amount of time to be in a particular job.

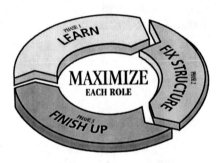

PHASE ONE: LEARNING

During Phase One in a role, your focus should be on learning your new job or role and developing a plan for what you want to accomplish and how you will do so. I like to spend my first thirty to sixty days researching the qualitative and quantitative aspects of my new role. During this time, I talk to as many people as I can about what is going on.

At this point, I try to understand the lay of the land. I focus on answering some specific questions:

- Who does what?
- How do things work?
- What are the inputs and outputs?
- What are the processes?

I focus on developing a hypothesis to guide my work in this role, and I try to avoid major decisions or making major changes to how things work in the first month.

After you have done your research, you will face many potential changes. The question is: *what do you have to do tomorrow, and what can wait?* It can be tempting to change everything all at once. Beware that if you try, you could fail badly. Worse, some changes may work and some may not. If you change too much at once, it can be hard to know which changes are succeeding and which are failing. Remember, too, that the work of the team cannot stop while you are trying new things.

This is a good time to write and publish your plan of action for the benefit of both your boss and your team. Try to show the plan in phases with clear objectives and outputs for each phase. Remember, both your boss and your team will view this closely and in great detail. Your boss will be looking to see if you understand what needs to be done, while your team will focus on the changes you are threatening to make! In both cases, try to do some preselling and clarify any assumptions before you start.

During the first six months in a new role, I set an objective to fix whatever is failing or will get in the way of later success. The hardest problems to deal with are the people problems. They can also take the longest to resolve. You may find that exiting a person from your team or your company can take many months. If the person is a significant problem for the team, the sooner you start, the better off everyone will be.

Around the six-month mark, you will get to the end of the first phase in this job or role. In complex organizations or roles, this phase can, of course, take much longer, *but be careful not to let it take more than a year.* If you move too slowly through phase one, your boss and your team may not think you are up to the role.

At the end of phase one, you will need to show that your approach is working and effective. Your team also needs to be under your direction and driving to achieve specific metrics.

Phase Two: Fixing Structural Problems

In almost every role or job, you will face some structural or long- term problems that need to be addressed. These long-term problems are often the result of too many years of inefficient or ineffective management. By the time you move into phase two, you should know what those problems are and how to fix them.

For example, people may be doing the right things, but existing processes might take too long and require too many approvals. These issues often exist not only within your team, but also between teams or processes.

Fixing these problems can take time. Most of these problems exist because no one has taken the time to address them—in other words, plodding along whilst ignoring them was just easier. In the worst cases, the problems are so ingrained that changing things can take years. Although you can probably get away with not fixing these problems, not doing so can lead you on a dangerous path. More important, these problems could hamper your team's performance.

A better approach is to show your boss what problems you face and how you plan to fix them. Remember, if you don't point out the holes that are causing the boat to leak, you will never get the credit for filling them.

Phase one is about identifying those holes. By the end of phase two, you should have filled them.

PHASE THREE: INNOVATING

By phase three, everything should be working properly, with all of the major problems addressed. At this point, you will have much more leeway to make structural changes. This is your chance to shake off any vestiges of Stuck-in-the Middle Management and break away from the pack by fundamentally rethinking how to do things.

Your focus should be on optimizing your approach and processes: is there a better way to do things? How can you increase productivity? In many roles, this phase is where the real innovation happens.

Innovation requires new thinking that focuses on what you want to achieve, not how you want to achieve it. This new thinking is unlikely to take hold immediately. You need to sell your ideas and goals to other managers and executives—and, sometimes, even your own team members—so that they will support and drive these changes.

In the end, successful leaders are judged more on what they accomplish during phase three than anything else they do in a given role. The work you do during phases one and two provides the foundation for your work in phase three. Don't make the mistake of taking shortcuts.

THE BOTTOM LINE

» Balance the need to get the most out of your role with the need to continue developing and breaking away from the pack.

NEXT STEPS

1. As you think about your current job or role,
    consider where you are in terms of the three
    phases—learning, fixing structural problems, and
    innovating. Then use that insight to build a plan to
    move on to the next phase.

2. If you are a manager, determine what role/
    phase each team member is in. Then develop an
    individualized coaching plan for each team member
    to help them move to the next phase.

NINE

GETTING PROMOTED FASTER

Earlier in this book, we discussed hunger and progressing in your career (Chapter 6). If you are interested in moving up into management or the executive ranks, you need to plan your career accordingly.

Even with the best career plan, you still may not be getting all of the career opportunities and promotions you feel you deserve. If that happens, you need to figure out why.

I remember having dinner with a younger colleague, Janet, who was frustrated that she was not getting promoted faster. Janet was doing everything right. She had chosen her progression of roles carefully and maximized the opportunity and results in each role. She had built a strong foundation of content. Her approach was sound. Her network inside and outside the company was extensive.

In short, she was doing what she was "supposed to do" to be well positioned for promotion. She was so frustrated with the situation and her current prospects that she was in danger of giving up and stalling out in the middle of the pack. She needed to do something about the situation.

To work through her concerns, Janet and I discussed the potential reasons why she was not moving ahead. This led us to three key questions:

1. Is it your company?
2. Is it your role?
3. Is it you?

Someone who has otherwise created a realistic schedule for promotions is likely to find the reason for a lack of promotion exists in the answer to one of those questions.

IS IT YOUR COMPANY?

If you are not getting promoted, you could be held back by the company's own limitations. For example, a small company is likely to have a limited number of promotions available. This is particularly true if you are the only one, or one of a few, who do a certain type of work. The company culture also may not be a good fit for your management and leadership style.

Customer or market needs can also drive companies to hire and promote some people rather than others. An engineer-centric company may have a tradition of promoting engineers into senior-level positions. If you are working in finance, your prospects with that company will be limited.

These are not necessarily good reasons for overlooking you as a candidate for promotion, but these reasons exist in many companies, and you have to recognize and deal with them. Quite simply, your company may not respect what you do or the skills you bring to the table enough to offer you promotion opportunities.

If this is true in your situation, you need to recognize that you may not get promoted in your company no matter how hard you work or how much you deserve it. Once you recognize the limited role this type of company can play in your career progression, you can decide whether to stay with the company, and for how long.

I have seen too many people become Stuck-in-the-Middle Managers out of frustration because they do not recognize how limited their prospects are at their current company, and are reluctant to move on.

This lack of promotion opportunity can also hit you as a manager when people who do essential work on your team finally decide that the company is not right for them. You can prevent these situations from happening in some cases by making sure you are doing annual career planning and development sessions with these employees.

Your focus during these sessions should be on understanding where these individuals are in their careers, and what their expectations are as to the next steps for them. If you find their expectations or assumptions are wrong, this is the time to review and correct those expectations or assumptions.

It is always better to do this during a career development session rather than during a separate review. When you engage in this type of discussion during an annual review, people tend to make a direct link between their performance and their prospects. Although there clearly is a link, people are likely to be more open when you separate these sessions.

IS IT YOUR ROLE?

You may be able to trace your limited promotion opportunities to the nature of your role. If you are a senior individual contributor who has spent years deepening your knowledge and experience in a particular area, it can be difficult sometimes to make the jump to a management role. You may have made yourself irreplaceable in this key role! No one is willing to move you elsewhere and lose access to your expertise.

Many people move into roles and jobs that limit their careers. For example, working on a team whose work is not considered essential to the business can hold you back. If people do not value the work you do, they will not raise you as a prospect in promotion conversations.

Some companies recognize these issues and encourage people to move around to different functions and departments as they build a career. If your company is not doing this, you can make these decisions for yourself. If you are a manager in engineering, spending some time in a sales role may be beneficial. This does not necessarily mean moving laterally to become a manager of sales, a position for which you are probably not qualified. Instead, you are more likely to get the go-ahead for such a move by taking on a less prominent role in the sales team that will still allow you to develop your sales content, but will likely have less risk for both yourself and your company.

As a manager, it is your responsibility to make sure that the roles you give to your own team members fit with those individuals' career expectations. When this is not possible, it is always better to be open and honest with the employee involved, and then manage the situation as well as you can. You do not want to make the mistake of trying to avoid confrontation (nontransparency; Chapter 7) by making promises to employees that you know will go unfulfilled.

IS IT YOU?

In my first job as a director, I promoted a member of my team to a management position. After I announced the promotion, another member of my team approached me to ask why I had not considered him for the job. I replied that I had no idea that he had wanted to be a manager. He had never mentioned that possibility, nor asked to be considered for a management role. Nor had he ever sought out advice on how to move up at the company.

The moral to that story is that *you need to let people know what you want.* If you want to be promoted and plan to work toward that goal, tell your manager or some other senior person who can help you achieve that goal. At the very least, these individuals can let you know when a new opportunity opens up. At most, they can provide advice and guidance on how to get that management role.

Apply for desired roles as they become open. It is your responsibility to know the company's openings, to ask questions about the role, and to apply your knowledge. Then approach colleagues and network to help you connect the dots and bring you into the hiring manager's view. If you find out about roles only after they are filled and closed, it signals you need to improve your network (Chapter 5).

All of this assumes that you continually acquire new content, expand your network, and hone your approach so that you are ready and well positioned for promotion (see Chapters 3, 4, and 5). If you are not taking those steps, this lack of preparation and development can be a key reason why you have not been promoted. If you do not have what is required to be a manager, someone else will get the job.

Of course, the lack of a promotion may not just be due to one of the above reasons; it may be due to a combination of two — or even all three! In Janet's case, the issue was a combination of the second and third reasons. She had made herself irreplaceable in her role, and resisted letting someone less qualified take over. So while she was doing all the right things to position herself to move on, the security of the job she knew always seemed to hold her back at the last minute.

For Janet and many others, the advice is simple: *At some point, you have to let yourself move on.* (As scary as that may seem…!)

THE BOTTOM LINE

» Work hard and position yourself to be in the right place at the right time — but if your current company keeps overlooking you for promotion, you must decide whether to stay or move on.

NEXT STEPS

1. Think through how long you have been in your role and how much longer you want to be there. Then find out your manager's expectations of you in your role, and convey to your manager your own expectations and career plans at the company.

2. If you manage people, make sure you are doing annual career plans for each one to ensure that you and they have synchronized expectations. Conduct these meetings separately from annual performance reviews.

TEN

BECOMING AN EFFECTIVE COACH

One of the best ways to break out of the pack and seem like a rising star is to share what you know with others so they become better at their jobs and at dealing with on-the-job challenges. As a manager, you are positioned to make a difference in the work lives of your colleagues and team members. You do this by being an effective coach. *A manager who is an effective coach is well on the way to becoming a 21st Century Executive.*

Coaching opportunities arise during your day-to-day work when you need to share your skill and experience to help an employee or team member complete a task. The vast majority of those responding to our At Work survey (85 percent) describe themselves as "good coaches" — but only half think other people are effective at coaching.

What makes a coach effective? We all know the Chinese proverb, "Give a man a fish and you feed him for a day. Teach a man to fish and you feed him for a lifetime." Put another way, *the best way to help someone is through coaching.* Sometimes, the person will ask you for coaching directly. At other times, you may become a coach because someone on your team or in your department or company needs specific help and your boss wants you to provide that help.

When you think about coaching someone, you likely have observed some specific weakness — a problem with key tasks, time management, confidence, or management approach—that the coaching relationship should address. Your goal as a coach is to help your students deal with the issues causing them to stall or fail in their role.

Let's look at an example where you might be asked to coach someone who does not work for you. Donna, a team leader, struggled with managing her team's work. Because her manager viewed Donna as a promising talent, the manager asked Bill, a leader from another team, to coach Donna on her performance issues. The coaching arrangement detailed what Donna needed to achieve.

Bill helped Donna determine how to achieve the expected results and deliver more work from her team. Donna had assigned all the complicated tasks to herself because she thought she could do them quicker (a key symptom of a Stuck-in-the-Middle Manager), but Bill advised Donna to delegate some of those tasks. Within a few months, Donna's performance had improved, as did that of her whole team, and Bill and Donna agreed to end the coaching relationship. However, the two continued to stay in touch informally, with Bill keeping tabs to make sure Donna's performance continued to improve.

This is an example of a typical coaching relationship, but it would be a mistake to believe that coaching only happens when things are broken or need fixing. Coaches can also help you to accelerate your career or increase your effectiveness. As such, a coach has some similarities to a mentor (see Chapter 11). However, a coaching relationship tends to be much more structured and formal than a mentoring relationship, and is often a work-based relationship.

As a coach, you help someone manage day-to-day responsibilities rather than providing the overall life and career advice a mentor does. A Human Resources department will often make sure that employees with high potential have "approved" coaches, and the department will track the subsequent interactions. By contrast, a mentoring relationship is not so formal or tracked. It also tends to be much broader and long-term.

A coaching relationship requires much more than everyday management and periodic performance reviews. In management, both the manager and the subordinate agree on the subordinate's objectives and goals, but how the subordinate achieves those objectives and goals is up to the subordinate. Coaching is more intensive, too, as it focuses on the details of how people do their job and how they plan to achieve their goals and objectives.

THREE KEY COACHING STEPS

The coaching process generally involves three key steps: preparation, discussion and, follow up.

Preparation. To ensure a productive coaching relationship, you need to *prepare*. Without preparation, the relationship will be less productive and potentially frustrating for the student. Preparation means learning about the work your student does, along with helping identify the root of the problem that the coaching relationship will address.

As a coach, you analyze your student's needs and situation. You view any tasks through the eyes of the student. You are probably the best choice for a coach if you have done the task(s) yourself. Coaching is not about your ability to do a task, but *your ability to help the other person.* Therefore, your preparation should be systematic, with facts, hypotheses, and examples of the employee's current behavior rather than relying on anecdotes and secondhand accounts of her performance. *What should they be doing differently?*

Often, I find it useful to think through a number of solutions to any problem before the coaching session starts. I even conduct some role-playing to prepare for this first conversation, by trying to think through the questions or objections that might come up.

Discussion. Once the coaching process begins, you focus on sharing information and actively listening to your student. In the process, you can look for the causes of the identified problems and begin to build action plans for improvement.

Beyond pointing out problems and flaws as a coach, you also need to focus on and be positive about what the student does well. Discussions should focus on how to be more effective rather than what the student has been doing wrong.

Discuss why the student's performance and behavior have limited his or her success and why that will continue unless he or she makes changes. While you can use yourself as an example, avoid making it sound like your approach is right and the student's is wrong. In most cases, the student's situation will be different from yours, and you need to discuss the task in that context. Remember, you are trying to get *the student* to do the task correctly, not prove that *you* know how to do it.

Consider ways for the student to practice what you discuss. Imagine you were coaching someone to hit a tennis ball. Telling the student how to hit the ball is good, but watching him or her do it would be better. You do not want the first time you see your student hit the ball to be on the job or, in this case, during a competitive match. Instead, you can use role-playing to see how the student deals with specific situations.

In all of your actions and discussions as a coach, you must be honest, act with integrity, and enable transparency.

Follow-Up. Once the coaching process begins, work with your student to ensure there will be an ongoing dialogue even after the structured coaching ends. Develop a follow-up plan. These discussions should focus on being supportive and constructive, but clear on what action the student needs to take to continue to improve.

In Donna's situation, the coach, Bill, should report back to the manager who asked for his help. Donna's manager needs to be clear on not only what Bill did to help Donna, but also on how Donna responded and what new skills she has learned and demonstrated.

If Donna ended up not learning anything, Bill must provide that input and feedback to the manager.

As a coach, you need to work with your student a number of times on the task(s) before giving up.

Coaching is not only a good way to fend off getting stuck-in-the-middle within yourself and within your team, it is hugely rewarding. I constantly look for opportunities to coach my team. Good managers incorporate coaching into their everyday work, making it a natural part of their management style. Just don't let your enthusiasm for coaching seep into your personal life. Your spouse or partner may be happy for you to coach your team, but he or she may not be as excited if you try to coach at home.

THE BOTTOM LINE

» The focus in coaching is on helping a student learn to handle any issues that negatively impact performance and results.

NEXT STEPS

1. When you are stuck on a problem, think about who is good at solving those types of problems and ask that person to coach you. Try to learn not only how to solve the problem, but also observe how an effective coach operates.

2. Next time you see someone doing something wrong, turn the situation into a coaching opportunity.

3. Next time you interview for a management or leadership role, ask the other person about his or her approach to coaching and compare it to yours.

ELEVEN

FINDING THE RIGHT MENTOR

A good mentor is an invaluable resource as you work to break away from the pack and shine. Having good mentors indicates that you have a great network — an excellent characteristic of a 21st Century Executive. Still, finding the right mentor can be a challenge.

A few years ago, I worked for a company that was acquired by Sun Microsystems. Following the deal, Sun asked me to work in the combined company. Undecided about whether to accept the opportunity, I consulted with one of my mentors.

My mentor was very supportive of the move to Sun. He noted correctly that, as a Silicon Valley company, Sun offered a very different organization compared to the companies I had worked for. He emphasized Sun's speed and innovative ways and the fact that having Sun Microsystems on my resume would be a very good thing.

Ultimately, I considered his input, what general skills I might develop in this new role, and the overall impact of taking on the role on my own personal portfolio. I accepted the job and worked for Sun for three years. I firmly believe that the skills and experience the job provided were instrumental in rounding out my character and helping my career growth. My experience with Sun helped significantly in my getting my next job.

DO YOU NEED A(NOTHER) MENTOR?

Everyone can benefit from having a mentor. I have worked with many mentors throughout my career, often more than one at a time.

You do need to think through why you want to develop a mentoring relationship: *what do you hope to get out of it?* Your answer(s) will help you identify potential mentors who can meet your needs.

Our At Work survey asked how many mentors the respondents had. Their answers indicated that almost one-third (31 percent) had no mentors. In fact, that was the most common answer to this question. Another 30 percent had only one mentor, while 25 percent had two mentors. Just 4 percent of those who responded claimed five or more mentors.

Most people seek a mentor because they know they need help in certain areas of their work or personal lives. Or they hope the mentor can provide contacts and a career boost.

What you want your mentor to do for you will help guide your choice.

If you want someone to help you improve in your current role, then you need to look for someone who has a background similar to yours, but with more depth and experience.

If you want to improve your management skills and avoid getting stuck in the middle and stalling our your career, you need to find an older manager with the necessary skills and experience and who recognizes the importance of being a 21st Century Executive.

Sometimes, you want someone to be your mentor simply because you respect the person as an individual and what he or she has accomplished. You think you can learn from him or her.

WHAT TO LOOK FOR IN A MENTOR

Finding the right mentor is similar to dating: you need to meet a lot of people, and not everyone will be the right fit. Before starting a mentoring relationship, talk a few times about both parties' expectations for the relationship.

In these conversations, determine if you both can find the common ground that is the foundation of any good mentoring relationship. (In other words, don't get married until you have dated for a while.)

When deciding to ask someone to be your mentor, you should consider three questions:

1. **Is this someone I can relate to, and does this person have what I need?** Sometimes, we expect a mentor to be a parental figure. At other times, the mentor serves as confessor. There are a variety of mentoring relationships. The core of any positive one should be *some commonality of experience and viewpoint.* Do not choose a mentor just because you think that person is someone important. *Get a mentor to whom you can relate.*

2. **Does this mentor have a background that is different enough from mine?** Although relating to your mentor is important, an effective mentor cannot be your mirror image. *You need someone whose experience is not exactly the same as yours.* Look for someone who has worked in a different function, role, department, country, or company — or some combination of these criteria. This will help you build a distinctively different relationship with your mentor.

3. **Will this person push me?** There is no point to having a *mentor* who agrees with everything you say and reinforces your own perceptions. *Intentionally, find someone who will push you and take you to the next level in your career and professional development.*

BUILDING THE RELATIONSHIP

A mentoring relationship is a sharing relationship. If you want to avoid being stuck in the middle of the pack, make sure the mentor you choose is not like a psychiatrist, but more of a management consultant to you. Here are some steps to build a stronger mentor relationship:

1. Think about this relationship not just in terms of what you can get out of it, but what you can (and are willing to) put into it.
2. Build a relationship based on trust and honesty. If you don't think you can do that, you may have the wrong mentor. For example, if you are worried about the potential repercussions of speaking frankly to a mentor who also works closely with you or your boss, you may need to look elsewhere for a mentor.
3. Think through how you will manage the mentoring relationship as well. Too many people make the mistake of assuming their mentors will drive the whole experience forward. However, you need to be prepared to follow up with your mentor and facilitate conversations.
4. Respect your mentor's time and make sure you use it wisely.
5. If the mentoring relationship is not working out, you need to consider your part in the problem and take whatever steps are necessary to make

things right—or end the relationship. It is all right to do that.

6. Consider whether your expectations for the mentoring relationship are reasonable. You cannot expect a mentor to do your job for you, or to give you all the answers. The best mentors ask good questions that help you develop your own ideas or spur you into action.

7. Don't limit yourself to one mentor. Different people bring different perspectives to your life. Having multiple mentoring relationships can provide you with a strong sounding board before you make decisions or take action on something. You do not have to meet with every mentor regularly. Some mentors may be people you check in with only every other year, while you may talk to another mentor weekly.

As we noted, mentoring can be like dating; therefore, breakups are inevitable. Although it may be easier to not say anything and just let the relationship die, that approach is not appropriate. The mentor has given you time and insights, probably for free. If you want to end the mentoring relationship, then you owe your mentor both an explanation and the honesty that goes with that. Be clear and factual. Thank the mentor for his or her time, and explain why you want to change the nature of the relationship. Remember, before you end a mentoring relationship, changing the frequency of your meetings from once a month to, say, once a year is also an option. Whatever you do, try to avoid burning bridges within your network.

The Bottom Line

» When picking a mentor, find someone you connect with and who has similar—but not exactly the same—job experience as you. Make sure they operate as your management consultant—not your psychiatrist!

Next Steps

1. Identify any areas in your profession where you are stalled or struggling, then approach someone whom you respect and who has similar experience, to see if he or she is willing to mentor you.

2. Initially, plan to meet with your mentor once a month until you see improvement in your problem spots.

3. If the mentoring relationship proves not to be working for you, thank your mentor first, then explain honestly and graciously why you are ending the relationship.

TWELVE

A VALUE PROPOSITION AS A CAREER TOOL

At the core of every business and career stands a *value proposition*. According to Wikipedia, "A value proposition is a promise of value to be delivered and acknowledged and a belief from the customer that value will be appealed and experienced. A value proposition can apply to an entire organization, or parts thereof, or customer accounts, or products or services."

If you are like most professionals, you do not spend enough time thinking about value propositions—your own, or those of your company. Indeed, a great sign that you are talking to a Stuck-in-the-Middle Manager is the long silence that ensues after you ask the person the question, "What is your value proposition?"

A 21st Century Executive can discuss in detail the importance of value propositions.

Whenever I see a product or service being badly marketed, I wonder if someone had really thought through the value proposition for the offering. If your value proposition is not done correctly, you cannot succeed in getting your offerings correctly positioned to your customers or markets.

If you want to understand product marketing or to be a product marketing person, you have to know how to write a value proposition. I use the knowledge of how to generate a good value proposition as part of the criteria in hiring a vice president of product marketing.

In this chapter, we are going to use the word "offering" to cover *any physical product or service* — e.g., the thing for which you are writing the value proposition. But it could also mean *you*, if you are developing a personal value proposition.

An effective value proposition focuses on the who, what, and the why of the offering on which you are working. If you are developing a value proposition for yourself and your career, your value proposition *defines who you are, what you can do, and why it is important to get to know you, work with you, and hire you.*

A more formal definition of value proposition is: an analysis of the quantified benefits, costs, and value that an organization can deliver to its customers and other stakeholders inside and outside of the organization. As we know, any time we can size or quantify our achievements, job interviews tend to go better.

WHY IS A VALUE PROPOSITION IMPORTANT?

A value proposition is an important part of selling our services, our businesses, and ourselves. If you can learn to develop and write a good value proposition, you can change everything about yourself, your company, and your environment.

The value proposition is the foundation of what you are selling — whether that is yourself, or a product. If you get your value proposition wrong, you undercut your overall value and pricing. In the long run, good products often fail because they have weak value propositions.

Here are two situations where a strong personal value proposition has helped me in my career:

1. When I make the case for a promotion or a new role, I articulate my value proposition clearly and succinctly.
2. When I interview for a job, I use my own value proposition to communicate my strengths and weaknesses. I focus on letting the other person know what they will be getting by hiring me, both the good and the not-so-good! For this to be effective, I make sure that my value proposition intersects with the company's hiring needs. Otherwise, I might take on a job or role that is not a good fit for my background or aspirations.

With a strong value proposition in place for yourself and for your company and its products, you know exactly what you need to communicate and what to manage in order to live up to that value proposition and to maximize results.

Strong marketing communications require an accurate value proposition. You also need an accurate value proposition when others are communicating your value on your behalf. This is particularly true if you are talking about a value proposition for an offering.

If you have sales people or channel partners, a clear and well-articulated value proposition will mean the difference between success and failure. If you don't think sales people fully understand the value proposition, having them summarize what they think the value proposition is can be an eye-opening experience. If they are close to articulating the value proposition correctly but not quite, that indicates one type of problem. If they are wrong or way off, something else is amiss. In most cases, the problems can be traced back to the value proposition itself. It has not been clearly thought through, and that results in an unfocused messaging.

Having a value proposition in place means that you have to live up to it through your actions. For example, a small business might define its value proposition as offering quality products. Yet, the company undercuts that value proposition if its staff is rude to its customers and if it does not offer quality service.

WHAT MAKES UP A GOOD VALUE PROPOSITION?

Developing a value proposition is a very structured process. You need to know where you are going in order to recognize any progress. This holds true whether you are developing a value proposition for yourself or for your company.

The ultimate goal is *to communicate the value proposition in four sentences or less.* If you cannot do that, you are not preparing yourself for success.

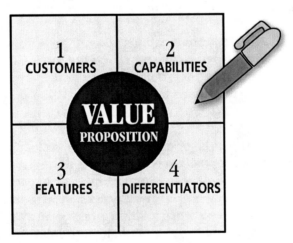

An effective value proposition needs to be real, specific, and measurably different. You can develop a strong value proposition by answering four questions.

1. Who are your customers?
2. What capabilities do they require from you?
3. What features do you offer?
4. What differentiates you from the competition? (Include the names of these competitors and quantified examples of why you are better.)

Unless you can answer these questions clearly, you will struggle to communicate the value of yourself or your product, and you are likely to miss with your marketing communications.

Before I launched the *3 Minute Mentor*, I developed a value proposition by responding to those questions with the following answers:

1. My customers are junior or middle-rank managers and executives who do not have a mentor;
2. I provide access to information and advice to help them manage their careers;
3. I offer a weekly short video and audio-based demonstrable mentoring advice;
4. My offering is unlike that of my competition because the *3 Minute Mentor* site is free and online, and allows users to gain access to information quickly and in short, easily retained segments.

This value proposition is effective because it reflects *the reality of* what the *3 Minute Mentor* currently is. It does not focus on what I hope the *3 Minute Mentor* will be at some point in the future. Such aspirational value propositions are not helpful. Compare that to the value proposition for this book: if you paid for a copy, or if someone else did, you know that the "free" element no longer applies. This book provides similar content to that on my site, but is packaged very differently, clearly plays to different needs, and therefore requires a different value proposition.

If you are developing a value proposition for your career as a middle manager, say, in the high-tech industry, the answers to the four questions outlined earlier could be:

1. My customers (current and potential employers) are technology companies with significant business in the pharmaceutical sector;

2. I provide proven management expertise, technical knowledge, and problem-solving and troubleshooting skills;

3. I offer team-level management capability that focuses on achieving key goals and delivering results within identified timelines;

4. I am unlike my competition because I have a proven ability to troubleshoot issues and get sidetracked projects back on schedule to deliver required results.

As noted, *avoid writing aspirational value propositions that are based on what you want to be true about your differentiation and what you hope will be true sometime in the future.* One way to ensure a realistic value proposition is to pledge not to write anything that you could not defend in court.

In your personal value proposition, you would not say that you have an MBA just because you want to study for one. By the same token, a value proposition should not state that the offering is half the price of the competitor's offering, unless you know that the pricing is definitely going to be at that level. *It is important to revisit value propositions when things change to ensure that it is still accurate and not based on wrong assumptions or changed realities.*

Your value proposition is not some kind of advertising copy. Do not spend too much time crafting the words or thinking of clever phrasing; others will do that when the time is right. *Your role in writing a value proposition is to be clear, simple, accurate, and honest.*

THE BOTTOM LINE

» A strong value proposition is critical to the success of any offering—be it yourself, or a product, or service—and needs to be realistic, simple, clear, and accurate.

NEXT STEPS

1. Write down your personal value proposition, then answer the four questions identified earlier in this chapter.

2. Think through a recent offering or project you were involved in that did not go as well as you had hoped. Can you find the value proposition for that offering? Write it down, and take it to your product communication and sales or channels teams. Can they see and appreciate what needs to be communicated? Together, identify what went wrong or awry before, then ask them to disseminate the specific value proposition of the offering.

3. Revisit the value propositions in your life every few months to make sure they still pertain and are accurate. If things have changed in your world, maybe time to look at your value propositions again.

SECTION II

MANAGING YOUR EFFECTIVENESS

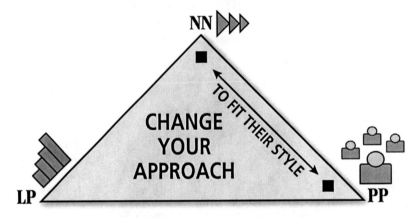

See more about Influencing Different Types of People in Chapter 23.

THIRTEEN

MAKING E-MAIL MORE EFFECTIVE

E-mail is a great tool that has become both a blessing... and a curse.

In the At Work survey, respondents said that more than half (54 percent) of the e-mails they receive are either average or poorly written. Of course, only 14 percent of those surveyed rated *themselves* as sending "average" or "poor" e-mails, whereas 86 percent believed they are either "good" or "extremely good" at writing e-mails. *Clearly, what we think we send is not what recipients believe they receive!*

When I started my career twenty-five years ago, e-mail was in its very earliest incarnation. We had to log onto a terminal hooked up to a mainframe computer that was difficult to use. Thanks to this setup, no one wanted to linger on the machine. It forced us to know what we wanted to communicate before we logged in and to get right to the point. We learned to write shorter, punchier e-mails.

Today, e-mail is ubiquitous, much easier to use, and abused. Ask any manager how many e-mails he receives in a given day and the number will easily be well over one hundred—and even a thousand or more in some cases. Nothing says, "I am stuck in busyness and unproductivity" more than having to dedicate hours to reading e-mails unrelated to what you are trying to accomplish.

E-mail, designed to be a productivity enhancer, has slowly had the reverse effect. The situation in one of my previous roles was so bad that my boss developed a document entitled, "What is important enough to use your boss's time?"

We could spend pages discussing what is wrong with e-mail these days. Instead, let's focus on how to turn e-mail back into an effective management tool for 21ˢᵗ Century Executives.

1. DON'T USE E-MAIL TO DO YOUR THINKING FOR YOU

Too many people use e-mail to capture their thought processes rather than their conclusions. If they type up every step of their logic and thinking, surely their great thought processes will interest the reader.

This approach only turns e-mail into something akin to learning calculus at school. When we did complex math at school, our teacher wanted to know the answer and how you got to the answer. Your logic flow was part of the answer and your grade.

Writing e-mails at work is not like doing calculus at school. Always assume no one is interested in how you came to your conclusion. They are only interested in what impacts them and their work, and anything on which they need to take action.

In some situations, you do need to show proof — for example, when you have been specifically asked for it. In another situation, you may be using e-mail as a briefing of some type because you will not have a chance to explain the ideas in person. Unless you are in one of these situations where you need to provide more detail, *keep it simple.*

Summarize your points precisely in your first paragraph. Follow with any required action. If the reader needs more detail or has questions, he can contact you to get that information.

You want the e-mail to make impact and ensure action, not gender praise for your writing skills.

Finally, evaluate whether e-mail is the best way to communicate your points. Consider whom you are trying to influence. Then choose the medium that your audience prefers. You cannot always influence people using the medium that is effective for you. You have to use the medium that is effective for them.

2. MAKE YOUR REQUEST CLEAR

When publishers lay out a newspaper, they place the most important news "above the fold." When you build a website, you don't want people to have to scroll too far down the page or do multiple clicks to get to the key content. You need to put key content right in front of them.

You should think the same way about your e-mails, especially when you are making requests. If you ask for something, always put that request, including names and dates related to the requested action, in the first two or three sentences of your e-mail. The best rule is to *include the call to action in the first line of an e-mail.* Do not assume that the reader will read far enough to see the request buried in all of the detail.

An e-mail that does not provide a clear reason or request for action is more likely to be set aside and dealt with later. As a result, you may not get what you need on time, or ever.

If your e-mail client allows you to turn e-mails into action by automatically scheduling meetings and follow-ups, leverage that capability.

3. LIMIT EMOTION OF ALL TYPES

When I managed a team of around four hundred people, at least once a week someone would say to me that there was "some big commotion brewing." Each time, one part of the team would be up in arms about what some other part of the team had said or done. I always asked how the person knew about this situation. Invariably the answer started with, "Well, there is this e-mail...."

Now, I use humor a lot in the workplace, both in meetings and in presentations. Humor can cut through a lot of noise when you communicate, and it can help a team rally around a common thought or issue. *Humor can have a very powerful role in the workplace – but it rarely belongs in e-mail.* This is especially true of sarcasm, which is very easy to misinterpret. The reader almost never gets what you are trying to communicate.

An e-mail forwarded to an outsider (a common occurrence these days) is even more likely to be misinterpreted, especially if there is humor involved. That individual will not have the proper context for the exchange or to understand your sense of humor. If someone misreads your intentions, even the most routine matter can blow up into a crisis.

Keep your e-mails factual and focused on the matter at hand.

4. USE THE "SAVE" BUTTON BEFORE THE "SEND" BUTTON

In theory, e-mail enables immediate communication. In reality, sending an e-mail is immediate—but receiving is not. People read e-mails as they want to and when they want to. If I want to tell you something fast and simply, using e-mail is much better than placing a phone call because chances are the e-mail is not interrupting anything. You can read the e-mail at your own leisure. Also, e-mails are time-stamped, so you can even be clear when it was sent.

With this in mind, just because you have written an e-mail does not mean you need to send every e-mail immediately.

The "save" button is much more useful in many cases than the "send" button. Let me explain why.

People annoy us all. People do stupid things. They might not mean to do them, but they do. Some people even revel in being controversial.

When these people use e-mail, many different problems can occur. Some people start e-mail streams without thinking of the consequences. Others like to use the "reply-all" function just to show everyone how smart they are. We have all seen e-mail streams become e-mail wars.

When we were young and got angry, grownups told us to count to ten before saying anything. *When you need to be cool and show that you have a levelheaded approach to problems, the last thing you want to do is send an e-mail when you're not in that frame of mind.* This is particularly true if the e-mail is something you wrote while feeling frustrated or annoyed.

If you are writing an e-mail about an emotional or difficult topic, such as a performance review or a follow-up to a contentious meeting, save the e-mail. Then, come back to it in thirty minutes or even the next day, and decide whether you want to send it in its current form or at all.

If you find yourself thinking twice about sending something via e-mail, don't send it at all.

5. USE THE PHONE

Although there are benefits to sending e-mails rather than making phone calls, my best tip on e-mails is when not to e-mail. In at least two scenarios, using the phone is always the better answer.

The first comes from the fact that we live in a litigious world. These days, an e-mail lasts forever, and there is no such thing as privacy in the workplace. In many cases, the laws and regulations governing publicly held companies require strict adherence to document retention rules. If you don't want someone else to read what you wrote, don't send it via e-mail.

I am not for a minute suggesting that you should be looking to get around laws or to act illegally. Your quest for honesty ensures that you do not want to break any laws. Nonetheless, in your business life, you will come up against situations where you don't know whether something is correct. It is not that you want to do the wrong thing—you do not want to be seen as even knowing what the wrong thing is.

For example, an auditor examining weaknesses in the company's training could use an e-mail in which you ask a question about how to use some process as proof of poor training practices. Conversely, picking up the phone to ask if you should follow a process gets the answer you need, alerts the colleague that training may be needed in that area, and does not leave a paper trail.

The second scenario is more critical. If the subject matter you want to discuss is important, sensitive and/or personal, a phone call or face-to-face discussion is always the better option.

THE BOTTOM LINE

» E-mail is a great tool for communicating, although we need to stop and think twice before hitting "send."

NEXT STEPS

1. Before you send your next e-mail, ask yourself what two things you can do to make that e-mail even more effective.

2. The next time you get an e-mail from a team member who is not as effective as it could be, coach the sender on how to improve that method of communication.

3. Have a discussion at your next team meeting on whether the "reply-all" feature is a good or bad thing to use.

FOURTEEN

GIVING BETTER PRESENTATIONS

Sometimes, it seems that the world is run by the PowerPoint presentation. Hang on, I think I have one here that makes that point....

Thanks largely to the ease of using PowerPoint, presentations have become a mainstay of the business world. Yet in the process, the effectiveness of these presentations has become almost an afterthought.

As noted in Chapter 13, the At Work survey indicated that we rate nearly half the e-mails we get as "average" or "poor" in our minds. The story for presentations is worse: the respondents rated six out of ten of the pitches we sit through as either "average" or "poor." But as with creating e-mails, we rate ourselves as giving "good" to "extremely good" presentations seven out of ten times.

PowerPoint is the tool of choice for a Stuck-in-the-Middle Manager. If you want to be an effective manager or 21st Century Executive, you must hone your presentation skills. Poorly thought out presentations with text-heavy slides and a monotone presenter are a mainstay of miscommunication. You don't want to be that type of presenter or that type of manager.

You must know your audience. Make sure your presentation is useful and relevant to them. I sat through one presentation in which the presenter asked for a larger budget. Unfortunately, I could not help him with his request because he did not work for me and I had no power to increase his budget. Moreover, the presenter actually had it in his control to solve his problem without anyone's help by rearranging his budget priorities and borrowing resources from other teams. The presenter had wasted my time and his own.

When I first started to build presentations — way before PowerPoint or even Freelance — I had to print out each page on sheets of acetate. These sheets were written on — *written on, not printed* — by an HP plotter. It took about twenty minutes to design the page, and another ten minutes to print it. This forced me to think carefully about what I wanted to say during a presentation and how to develop the fewest and most effective slides to support those points.

In modern presentations, we need to refine and hone our skills. Here are five ways to improve them.

1. SHORTER AND SIMPLER IS BETTER

Longer is not better when making a presentation. Shorter and simpler is. Don't structure your presentation according to the number of charts you have. Structure it based on what you need to say to make your case.

All communication is about sending and receiving. You need to send a message and you need the other person to receive it. When you make the message or the presentation too complex, long or confusing, you risk that your message will be neither received nor understood by your audience. This disconnection can account for why we *think* we give such good presentations — and other people view most presentations as average to poor.

Venture capitalist Guy Kawasaki suggests using the 10/20/30 rule — 10 charts for a 20-minute presentation using 30-point font. Taking this approach will help you focus on communicating the most important information in a simple way. Remember: *being simple is not the same as being simplistic.*

When I see people being too verbose in charts, I suggest they build what I call "a six-pack presentation." A *six-pack* relies on only six pages, including the title and summary pages, to make the necessary point. The key is limiting each page to only one major point and its proof-point. This technique not only has a slimming effect on the presentation, but it also forces the presenter to focus on the key point and not get lost in minor subpoints.

When developing each slide, avoid excessive text. You want to present information to your audience — not have them read it off the slide. PowerPoint is not a word processor, so don't use it as one.

Focus on using images to make your points. A carefully chosen image combined with charts, graphs, tables, and other ways of showing data clearly can save you many words.

2. MAKE YOUR CASE

You give presentations *for a reason*. You need to communicate about a specific issue, make a case for action, or update your team or management. The moment you say that your presentation is "for information," your audiences will stop listening. I even had a boss who would respond to such a statement with, "Okay, leave it behind, and I can read it when I have time" — not something the presenter ever wanted.

In some cases, you may find that your audience only pays attention to the first slide or two, then either tunes you out or assumes what the rest of the presentation will say. When that happens, you have lost your audience.

To assure the audience gets the message you want to send, keep things simple and uncomplicated. Make the story line or your request easy and clear enough so that it is unmistakable. Don't make your audience look for your point.

In some cases, I put my request on the first page rather than leaving it to the last page. That puts the message right up front. I want people in attendance at the presentation to know from the beginning the objective for my talk.

When you make your case as early in the presentation as possible, do so clearly, unemotionally, and factually. These are the four elements to focus on:

1. A factual analysis of the current position;
2. Current problems and root causes that may not be obvious to everyone;
3. Possible alternatives;
4. A proposal laying out your preferred course of action backed up by data, such as number of people, dollars involved/saved, etc.

3. PRESENT TO THE AUDIENCE, NOT TO THE CHARTS

The worst presentations are those in which the presenter stands at the front of the room and reads the slides. A colleague once gave a presentation with his back turned to the audience the entire time while he read off the words on his slides. To say this damaged his reputation among the audience members is an understatement.

When you ignore the audience in favor of your slides, you send a clear message that you are more impressed with your words than whether the audience gets the message. If you want your audience to read the slides and charts, just send them the PowerPoint deck and avoid the hassle of making the presentation.

A better approach is to think through the key message for each slide before you do the presentation. Focus your comments on answering the question, "What is the point of this slide?"

Finally, it is important to practice your presentation skills. People focus more on how you present your information rather than on what you say. The speed at which you speak, the strength of your voice, and the language you use always has an effect on how the audience takes in your words. As the size of your audience increases, these elements of your presentation become more important.

As a manager, you should always offer your team the chance to rehearse their presentations with you first. This has three key benefits:

1. By practicing the presentation, you gain confidence as the presenter;
2. By practicing the presentation out loud, you often find charts that either do not make the designated point or are unnecessary;
3. By practicing the presentation, you may realize it is poor, giving you a chance to intercept it and revise it before it goes any further than you.

4. DON'T ASK FOR SOMETHING
THAT IS UNDER YOUR CONTROL

The most important thing you can do as a presenter is to *keep your audience's needs in mind*. If you have to tell them something that they need to know, make sure you clearly communicate your message. If you are simply telling them what you think they should hear, chances are good that you are not going to be effective.

A presentation should not focus on what you already control — your budget, your people, and so on. It should focus on one of two things: (1) letting people know what you are planning to do with the resources and the authority you have; or (2) asking for additional resources and authority to achieve your objectives. In the latter case, you focus on making your case effectively, efficiently, and positively.

5. KNOW HOW TO ANSWER ANY QUESTIONS

It is better if people wait until you finish your presentation to ask questions. Sadly, audiences are rarely that helpful, so you need to be prepared both to interrupt your flow and to get back to the point when you are done answering the question. *Whatever you do, do not look annoyed by the interruption.*

Here are three simple situations and their appropriate responses:

1. If the answer to the question is the point of the chart on display, get to the point quickly. Avoid saying, "I'm coming to that," and then taking too long or forgetting to get to it. The audience does not necessarily care how clever you are, just what the answer is.

2. If the answer is on a different page or chart, move or refer to that page. Answer the question and go back to where you were. Some people worry that the interruption will derail them and will try to put off the questioner until later. The problem with doing that is that the questioner may feel you ignored them, even if in the end you did not. Should you decide to delay answering the question, when

you get to the page with the answer, refer back to the question.

3. If the answer is nowhere in your presentation, then either give the answer, or offer to come back later with a response. It's better to admit you "do not know" than to appear to be making an answer up that may be wrong.

The objective is always to communicate your point or your message. Good questions can help you do that, as they give you a chance to remake and refocus your point. Oftentimes, bad questions also can give you that opportunity. Bad questions, although it is best not to describe them as such, provide an opportunity for a dialogue and to ask for clarification. In that discussion, you can come to understand why the person is asking the question and redirect your answer to make it more specific. Typically, you are allowed to clarify the question with the asker. This kind of interaction, done well, makes your presentation more interesting for the audience.

At all points, avoid saying, "Good question!" While there is nothing wrong with saying that from a practical standpoint, some people end up saying that in response to every question. In that case, your response sounds fake or suggests that you are playing for time to think of an answer. If necessary, say it in your head (i.e., not out loud), and then respond.

THE BOTTOM LINE

»   The most effective presenters think about what their audience needs to hear, and practice offering the information simply, efficiently, and effectively first.

Next Steps

1. Review your last major presentation from the perspective of an audience member, not as the presenter.

2. Next time you have to make a difficult presentation, build a "six-pack version" first. That might be the one you may ultimately use.

3. Run a team competition to see who can do the best at communicating a complicated thought using the simplest chart.

FIFTEEN

SIMPLE RULES FOR TIME MANAGEMENT

As you move up into management and more senior positions in your career, managing your time becomes more important—and more difficult. Strong time management skills can mean the difference between future success and stalling your career, and being a 21st Century Executive or a Stuck-in-the-Middle Manager.

Employees struggling in stalled careers often arises out of poor time management. I have seen too many team members who work longer hours than necessary because they do not manage their time well.

One team member in particular stands out. His workload was no heavier than that of his peers. However, he was consistently putting in many more hours per week than they did. After talking with him about the situation, it became apparent that the problem was how he managed his time as he moved through his duties. He spent a lot of time spinning his wheels, looking for material and information that was haphazardly filed, and working on things that were not within the scope of his role or his authority. The result was his career was stalling out because of his lackluster performance.

You can easily find yourself in a similar position as you become better at your job and take on more responsibilities — because of all the commodities in the world, *time* is the only one of which you cannot get more. You can often get a larger budget. You can often hire more people. No matter what, there always will be only twenty-four hours in a day.

While some people find value and inspiration in detailed time management approaches such as *Getting Things Done*, Franklin Covey, and the time management courses their employer inevitably offers, such tools do not work for everyone.

I have always found such tools and courses to be interesting and motivating at first, but after using these tools day in and day out, I find their approaches to be too complicated to remember or follow consistently. In the days when people carried a paper diary or calendar, such tools fit well into many people's workflows. Today, lives revolve around a computer or smartphone. While many time management tools have made it to the twenty-first century, those tools are harder to integrate into today's workflow. Thus, out-of-sight is often out-of-mind with these tools.

Knowing that I needed some sort of system to manage my time and my inflow and outflow of information, I identified five simple rules for managing my time and work effectively.

1. COMMIT TO SHORTER MEETINGS

Managers spend a lot of time in meetings. *If your time is short, spend less of it in meetings.*

You can make a policy decision to limit meetings to thirty minutes, unless the requestor makes a case for more time. This should not be difficult for people to accommodate. Most meetings require about thirty minutes, but people book meetings in hour-long increments out of habit or to make sure that they have enough time to deal with anything that comes up during the meeting. If you use Microsoft Outlook or something similar, set your default meeting time to thirty minutes, not an hour.

Larkin Kay, a former colleague who now runs her own consulting business, tells me that by keeping meetings to thirty minutes, she can use the other thirty minutes of that hour to process what happened or needs to happen. You can also use this block of time to prepare for the next meeting or to catch up on e-mail. She also schedules time in her calendar to do work. *If you don't block off time to work, then other things can get scheduled in those spots.*

Preparing ahead of time is essential to having successful shorter meetings. My philosophy, which has been borne out in real life, is that *anything you can do in an hour you can do in thirty minutes* if you prepare well enough.

The best way to keep meetings short is to keep them focused and on track. I begin every meeting by clearly stating the objectives for the meeting. I often use a little humor and ask the question, "We are gathered here today because...?" Once we have an answer, everyone knows what they are gathered to achieve. In addition, if someone wanders off topic and brings up something unrelated to the objective, it's easy to postpone or table that topic until another time or another meeting.

2. WRITE YOUR TO-DOS IN A DIFFERENT PLACE THAN YOUR MEETING NOTES

While we may not use expensive time and note management systems, most people still take notes during meetings. A few do this on a PC or smart device, but most of us use a paper-based notebook or notepad. One important time management trick I've learned over the years is a simple one: keep your to-do list separate from your meeting notes.

Many of my colleagues make a to-do list in meetings among their overall meeting notes. If this information were interspersed with my meeting notes, I would have to go back through pages and pages of notes to find my various to-dos.

By keeping meeting notes and the to-do list separate, I more easily cross things off as I complete them and generally keep tabs on what I have done and what I still need to do. I used to weight each item based on its importance until I found myself spending too much time trying to judge which items were more important when all of them needed to get done.

Keeping notes and to-dos separate makes them much easier to manage as long as you mark the ones you have completed. You also should commit to going back over your to-dos once a week and making sure they are to-dones.

3. DESIGN A WORKFLOW FOR YOUR E-MAIL

Even if you do not use your PC to take notes, chances are good that you use it for e-mail, which is probably both the bane and boon of your work life. The value of quick and easy communication is offset by the constant flow of messages. Getting hundreds of e-mails each day means that the urgent and critical are mixed in with the irrelevant and mundane.

To make sure e-mail helps more than it hinders, build a workflow system for your e-mail that brings your inbox down to a manageable level. I focus on ending each week with less than a page of e-mails that require action. I delete or file the rest of the e-mails.

The most efficient people I have ever worked with have similar systems. They manage their e-mail workflow with the same diligence that they apply to work flow for processes or thoughts. Moreover, these people apply these rules and use these tools consistently.

Here is how I manage my e-mail workflow:

1. Delete all irrelevant e-mails immediately.
2. File all e-mails that are for information only as soon as you read them.
3. Create a specific area or folder for e-mails that require later action or need to be read at some later time. Typically, I use names like "AA-Action," "AA-To Do" or "AA-To Read." (I use the "AA" to make sure these items appear on top of an alphabetical list.)
4. Make sure your inbox only contains the e-mails that relate to things that require actions from you or issues you need to watch and monitor.

My system may not work for you. Do find a way to keep e-mail manageable using a system that makes sense to you, that feels comfortable, and that you will use consistently.

I had one member of my team who used to have thousands of e-mails in his inbox. I asked him if he found that depressing. No, he said, it was his filing system. Actually, as I helpfully pointed out, it was the complete absence of a filing system, but if that's the way he wanted to work, then that was his call. Personally, I could not think of anything more depressing than to have my PC tell me I have two thousand unread e-mails.

4. HAVE A GOOD FILING SYSTEM ON YOUR COMPUTER

Just as you need to keep e-mail manageable, you also need to manage the information on your computer. Here are three ways to do this:

1. Create an organized filing system for documents, e-mail, folders, and other data. Rather than filing by date, I have found that filing by subject or

person makes things easier to find and track when I need them.

2. Once your system is up and running, use it consistently.
3. Don't let your filing get backed up. File e-mail, documents, and presentations as you receive them.

When you can quickly get your hands on what you need, you have more time to do your work and to focus on the issue at hand rather than the mess on your computer desktop.

Over the last several years, I have worked for a number of different companies. At each company, I used the same basic filing system on my PC. Some of the directories you would find on my standard PC include Analysts, Competitors, Press, and Market Research.

For me, my filing system and how to find things are now second nature. If you create the rules, your system will become second nature to you, too.

5. DELEGATE AND ESCALATE

You don't have to do everything yourself. In fact, there are certain things your company and senior management do not want you to do. You can't be an effective manager if you spend your time doing the work you should have given to someone else. There are people who can help you if you trust them to help you do your work.

You also can't be an effective manager if you try to solve problems or make decisions that should have been escalated to someone with the proper knowledge and authority.

Delegation and escalation are among your most important time management tools. Learn how to use them well. See

Chapter 24 for more on escalation and Chapter 30 for more on delegation.

THE BOTTOM LINE

» The secret to time management is planning what you do and focusing on getting the priority work done.

NEXT STEPS

1. Go through your calendar for the last month and count the number of meetings you had. How many could have been done in half the time with more planning? How much time would it have saved?

2. For one week, do not allow any meetings that last more than 30 minutes. Assess where that guideline worked, and where it didn't.

3. Review your e-mail and PC filing systems. Are they easy-to-use and consistent?

SIXTEEN

MANAGING STRESS

To be a successful manager, you must learn to manage and minimize your stress levels as much as possible. Your organization, your bosses, your people, your customers, your work, and your personal life all seem to conspire to raise your stress level. If you think you don't have any stress in your life, you are either unbelievably lucky — or missing much of what is going on around you.

In the At Work survey, 62 percent of the respondents said they are either "good" or "very good" at managing stress. What those individuals (and you, the reader) need to understand is that there are two types of stress: the type you admit to and the type you do not admit to. I used to think I did not have any stress. I know others who have said the same. I no longer believe that is true.

There are sound medical reasons for reducing stress. We all want to live longer. Stress not only affects you, it also affects those around you. They have to live with you, too. The people I know who have the most stressful lives often have the least happy lives. Their family and friends tend to suffer, too. Excessive stress can also lead people toward career stall-outs. They stop trying to maximize their effectiveness in order to just make it through the day.

DEALING WITH STRESS

I have come to recognize those of my colleagues and friends who have learned out how to manage stress, and those who have not. Over the years, through working with friends and colleagues, I developed these six habits to reduce and manage my own stress levels.

1. TAKE VACATION DAYS

Early in my career, one of my bosses threatened me with a bad rating and no bonus if I didn't take all of my vacation days. So the need to get away and recharge was a lesson I learned early on. It continues to be an important one.

That means really taking a vacation. Taking long weekends or going somewhere else, but still doing calls and e-mails doesn't count. Let's be honest: even if you are out of the office, checking in with the office, doing work, and attending conference calls is still working. You cannot recharge over a long weekend, especially if much of the time is spent traveling. I believe that you need to take at least ten days off in a row to really relax. Giving your body and mind time to relax and spending time with the important people in your life are crucial to personal and professional success.

Some people claim they have no choice but to stay connected to the office. They argue that their companies expect them to be available even when on vacation. While in some cases that might be true, I have found that many people who call into conference calls while on vacation invariably could have had someone else on their teams participate in the call. They just want to know what's going on. They might as well have been at work.

Just as you organize your work, you have to organize your life so you can take time off. I took two weeks off to get married about eight weeks before one of the biggest projects of my life.

I was able to do that because I knew I could rely on a great team that was synchronized and well-organized.

2. TRAVEL SMART

Few things in business are more stressful these days than business travel. If business travel is a significant part of your work, develop habits and requirements to reduce travel-related stress as much as possible. I have an understanding with my wife that if I leave on a business trip Monday morning, I get back by Friday so that I am home for the whole weekend. Even though I am not always successful in accomplishing this, having this stated goal makes my being home for the weekend much more likely.

Everyone is different. Figure out what works best for you and structure your travel schedule accordingly. Make your travel fit your lifestyle, not the other way around. Some people would rather get to their destination a day early to ensure a good night's sleep and to avoid rushing to the airport for an early flight. Others prefer to carry very little onto the plane and plan their schedules to allow time for checking and picking up a bag at baggage claim.

The key is to think about how you travel and the restrictions you put on yourself. Make sure your habits reduce your stress rather than increase it. Instead of continuing to do the same thing out of habit, determine if your current approach works for you: does it allow you to travel and work productively? Are you taking steps to make travel more convenient and, in the process, making it more stressful—for example, by struggling with a carry-on bag instead of checking it? Even paying baggage check fees can be worthwhile if it eliminates that headache from your day.

There is also a question of what you should do while you are in planes, trains, and automobiles. I know many, including me, who use the time on planes to do big projects (writing, reading, etc.), for these are more easily done without the constant interruptions of the office. Often when I travel during personal time, like weekends and in the evening, I prefer to read or watch movies. You need to give yourself time off, too.

3. DON'T START AND END YOUR DAY WITH E-MAIL

Writer and speaker Tim Sanders suggests never star ting or ending your day handling e-mail. If you think about it, this makes very good sense.

Most e-mail does not bring good news. It brings problems and troubles into your workday. Better to wait to deal with those things until after breakfast. Also, don't read e-mail before going to bed. Even if someone sends you an e-mail late in the day, they do not necessarily expect you to deal with the issue involved right then and there, so why read about that problem right before going to sleep? Spending the first and last hour of the day with someone you love, rather than with a problem-laden e-mail, is much less stressful.

4. DON'T WORRY ABOUT WHAT YOU CAN'T fix

Probably the most challenging factor for some people to accept is that they can't do everything. To keep your stress levels manageable, you need to recognize that there are some problems that you can fix and some problems that you cannot. There is no point in worrying about the things you can't change or fix.

At the same time, you need to let situations play out. My wife always says, "Somewhere between as good as it can be and as bad as it can be is where it will be." Others may put it in slightly different terms, like, "It is what it is," and "Let it play out," as a way to remind themselves that they cannot control and fix everything.

These philosophies are a great way to have an "out," but make sure you do not use them as an excuse. Don't say that something "is what it is" if you have the ability to influence it. If something is going wrong in your company, you need to focus on dealing with the problems and issues that are within your control.

5. MAKE DECISIONS WITH YOUR HEAD,
BUT EXECUTE THEM WITH YOUR HEART

In life and business, you have to do difficult things and make difficult decisions. Sometimes, those difficulties involve having no other choice than to cause bad things—like a layoff or firing— to happen to good people. *Business requires difficult decisions.* If you do not want to make those decisions—such as the decision to lay off part of the workforce—then do not take on a leadership role.

Although you may not have a choice about taking a specific action, how you execute that action is often up to you. An early mentor in my career gave me an important piece of advice: *make every decision with your head, but execute it with your heart.* Out of all the advice I've gotten throughout my career, I believe this to be among the most important.

How you communicate bad news and how you behave and listen in the aftermath is up to you. I know I sleep better at night when I execute difficult decisions with my heart.

I remember coming to the decision to fire someone. The decision was right for the company for many reasons, but it was also right for the individual. Having made that decision, I then focused my efforts on allowing that person to leave the company with as much dignity as possible. This allowed the individual to say goodbye to colleagues and customers, and to have some closure to the situation. To this day, I still maintain a good relationship with this person even though I had to fire him at one point.

Believing and living this philosophy are not always easy. This will be particularly true when you work with other people who do not know or share this approach. Some will opt for short-term financial gain for the company rather than the long-term better interests of their people. If they argue that their action is more "financially prudent," the question you can ask yourself is whether that is really true. Will the impact of the decision have a material impact, or are they just being mean? If you believe a decision is rooted in meanness rather than prudence, it is your choice whether to say something.

Sticking to your principles is never easy, but we all want to have a clear conscience. Only psychopaths do not worry about the implications of their actions. Unless you fall into that category, make sure your heart is involved at the right time.

THE BOTTOM LINE

» There are some things you can control and some things that you can't. Learning the difference between the two will help you to sleep better at night.

NEXT STEPS

1. Write down a list of the things that add the most stress to your life.

2. Pick one of these each quarter, and put a plan in place to minimize its effect.

3. Commit to taking a vacation in the next year that has you out of the office for ten working days and not reading your work e-mails every day!

SEVENTEEN

Managing a Budget

Do not stop reading this chapter because you think its content is too obvious, particularly when 71 percent of us believe that we are either "good" or "extremely good" at budgeting, according to the At Work survey. While it might seem that anyone who has managed a bank account for more than six months or lived away from their family home for more than one day might know how to budget by instinct, the truth is that most people do not.

I am constantly amazed by the inability of people who have been working for many years to manage a budget. In some cases, they just do not think about budgeting. In other cases, they do not view the company's money as "their money" and do not see the need to be careful with it. That mindset belongs to an executive from a previous generation, and not a modern, integrity-based 21st Century Executive. *Not managing your budget is a classic way to stop your career in its tracks or derail it entirely.*

As you move up in the management ranks, you will be responsible for spending larger and larger amounts of money. Aside from the organizational chart, some managers gauge their place in the company's hierarchy according to the size of their budgets.

With management authority comes the responsibility of managing corresponding budgets effectively even when it is very unpopular to do so. As a senior marketing executive, I once had to cut all of the marketing budgets under me by a double-digit percentage. Clearly, this was going to be very unpopular with the hardworking marketing team, but the action became necessary when I saw a great deal of waste and noncompetitive bidding going on within the team.

The cuts caused the shock and anger one would expect. We had countless meetings where people told me that the cuts would be the end of their department; they could do nothing on such small budgets. What I wanted and needed to do was to send a clear message about the importance of managing the company's money. Quite simply, we were spending too much for too little return.

To achieve the savings, I asked them to replace any single supplier relationships and put out contracts for competitive bidding. Any contract of $100,000 or more required three bids, and the teams had to use the company's global sourcing team to get the most competitive quotes.

Following the cuts and the new rules, I had some pushback from my managers. We solved that problem by taking two steps. First, we cut their budgets and, second, we told the managers that they could keep any additional reductions they got from the competitive bidding process to reinvest in their teams.

At the core of the problem was the question of whose money everyone was spending. For years, everyone had referred to budgets as "our money." However, we all had to understand that the money saved, like the rest of the budget, did not belong to the managers or me. It belonged to the company and its shareholders.

Much harder for some to accept was the fact that any money in our budgets that we did not need should go to shareholders as profit or to invest in another area of the company. Spending money just because it is in your budget is not effective business management.

SMART BUDGET MANAGEMENT

How you approach budgeting and how you manage your budget is very visible to your direct reports, your peers and senior management. It is important that you do it well.

When you are new to management, you may not have experience managing a budget. Here are the basics and some do's and don'ts to consider.

1. THE BASICS OF BUDGETING

Most organizations have many types of budgets, and each is often managed differently from company to company.

Here are the four key types of budgets:

1. A headcount or functional budget that covers the people costs of your team or your department;
2. Program budgets for money spent on operations and projects (and typically in an amount in your currency and even a quarterly allocation or skew);
3. A sales incentive budget with money designed to motivate sales or a channel as agreed and approved with the Sales and Human Resources team;
4. A capital budget for spending on assets, although this is to be carefully managed and monitored by the finance team. This budget also comes with a quarterly plan that shows you in which quarter of the year, or even which month, the money should be spent.

In total, these may all appear to be "your" budget. In reality, you must manage each of these budgets differently because the accounting treatment for these budgets differs. Some budgets involve operating expenses, some affect gross margin, and some affect net profit.

If you are managing a team, your finance team may give you a headcount budget that is both a people number and a financial cost. You may need to manage both. If you just manage to the headcount number, then you may tend to hire the best people you can. If you just manage to the cost or budget number, then you may tend to hire a larger but less expensive team. *Managing to both requires you to strike a balance.* In all cases, the expense is part of the operating expenses of the company.

If you want to hire some contractors to support your budget, you need to determine if that cost is part of the headcount expenses or part of the program budget. There are rules for these issues so you would need to talk to your finance and Human Resources teams to make this call.

If you buy equipment instead of hiring people or instead of replacing some people, those costs come out of your capital budget. Questions about whether those expenditures will reduce your headcount budget and whether depreciation will be charged to your program budget or to a separate company account need to be answered by your finance team.

As noted, budgets like capital expense budgets should be allocated by quarter, or even by month of the year. While you can often get program or functional budgets moved between quarters or months, capital budgets are often more restrictive. Again, check with your finance team.

2. THE DOS

Here are some key things to do when managing your budget:

Commit to keeping to your budget. Doing so is a sign of integrity. When it comes time to make promotion decisions, senior management will look closely at your budget management.

Know your budget and how often it is updated. Your approach to managing the budget should depend on how often you get updates and on how much is still available to spend. If you only get told your team's travel expenses once a quarter, you need to do a good job of estimating monthly costs. If your finance team can give you a monthly number, you can pass that information on to the team, which then requires you to do less tracking. Regardless, *you should always have a view of where your expense line is.*

Develop an amicable working relationship with finance. The finance department's job is to manage the company's finances, so treat these professionals as a resource rather than as an antagonist. Finance can help you understand the accounting treatment of your budget and how that impacts your expenditures. Finance can also tell you who keeps tabs on that budget, which is important information to have. Have an agreed-upon monthly or quarterly review process with an agreed-upon and organized set of repeatable content.

Make sure the people who are spending your budget understand the importance of budget management and how the budget works. If you think of this as "your" money, you will manage it like it *is* your money! In addition, you will expect those who spend it for you to do the same. Having those individuals understand the way the budget works will help your team members make better and more informed decisions.

3. THE DON'TS

Here are some things to avoid when managing your budget:

Don't overspend your budget. If your budget is not large enough for your needs, ask for more. If you are unable to get a larger budget even after stating the business case for those funds, you must make do with your original allocation.

Don't spend what you don't need. There is no business reason to spend your entire budget if you do not need to do so. You can always give back the leftover money. Although this might impact the size of your next budget, explain the reason for the excess and ask for an exception so that future budgets are unaffected.

Don't expect others to make up the difference if you overspend your budget. Your job is to manage your budget. Another manager might agree to transfer his budget for any number of reasons, but it is not his responsibility to do so. If someone does agree to a transfer to cover extra spending, it is important to get agreement from finance for the transfer, and to plan and have a paper trail for the transfer.

Personally, I have always treated keeping to my budget as a sign of my integrity, and I take that very seriously. Employees and colleagues who overspent their budgets never lasted very long on my teams.

I am not alone in this thinking. In fact, people who overspend their budgets don't survive in most companies.

THE BOTTOM LINE

» Start to think of the money in the budget as belonging to the company, not to you — meaning, don't spend money just because it is in your budget.

NEXT STEPS

1. List the types of budgets you manage and make sure you know how they will be accounted for.

2. Invite someone from finance to come to your next team meeting and ask that individual to present how the company manages its budgets and who looks at what and when.

3. Create a monthly or quarterly budget review package with finance; then review it with your team.

EIGHTEEN

EMPOWERING YOURSELF

There is an old joke in which an employee says to the boss, "If you wanted me to use my initiative, you should have told me so."

The same joke could be told about empowerment. The strangest questions I have encountered as a manager are, "How can I empower my team?" and "How can I convince my manager to empower me?" These questions are the siren's call of one Stuck-in-the-Middle Manager to another!

A lack of understanding of empowerment is one of the most classic signs that you are stalling out and lacking ownership of your job and career. If you want to be a 21st Century Executive, you absolutely need to understand all you can about *empowerment.*

The simplest definition of *empowerment* is: giving power to someone else. I don't care much for this definition because it seems very top-down and misses a larger context.

In social terms, *empowerment allows people to gain control over their own lives.* No one gives them that power; they take it and empower themselves.

Dr. Martin Luther King, Jr. did not wait for anyone to give him the authority or permission to protest Jim Crow laws and to eventually lead the civil rights movement. He took on that authority over time and empowered himself to act.

Even if you are not a civil rights leader, you do not need to wait for someone to give you authority or permission to do your job. *You just start doing it until someone tells you not to.*

In business terms, when you give someone power to do something or someone gives that power to you, that is less about empowerment than it is about delegation.

In other words, you cannot empower your team. Your team needs to empower itself. Your boss cannot empower you. You must empower yourself.

WHAT IS THE ROLE OF EMPOWERMENT IN YOUR CAREER?

Empowering yourself from a career perspective comes with some risk. But let's face it: anyone who aspires to a management role must be comfortable with taking charge and taking intelligent risks. *As you move up the management ranks, the ability to empower yourself and to take risks becomes even more critical.*

Most people want to do the right thing on the job. They want to do their jobs well, work well with others, and complete their tasks on time. As people move up the management ranks, these three elements remain important, but the choices they must make to achieve these become more complicated.

Managers generally do not receive, and should not expect to receive, detailed instructions on how to do their jobs or accomplish their objectives. Their bosses expect them to figure that out themselves, or to empower themselves to do their jobs.

If you lack specific resources to complete a task, you need to identify those resources and figure out how to obtain them.

You do not ask anyone's permission; you just do what you need to do.

This is where the risk and the reward of empowerment come in. If you are successful because you empower yourself, you are likely to move up in the ranks. This, in turn, requires you to embrace empowerment even more. In fact, the higher you rise, the greater your risk becomes (less job security) and the greater your reward (higher pay and recognition).

THE RISKS OF AVOIDING EMPOWERMENT

It is important to note that *not* empowering yourself also has risks. Managers who are reluctant to empower themselves are not likely to get far in their careers.

If you are uncertain about something, ask for help or input— but keep in mind that this is not the same as waiting around for instructions.

If you want to be in a position of power and want to make a difference, then you have to *take action*. When you reach senior levels of management, the risk of not empowering yourself can be fatal.

If I, as a chief marketing officer, had ever gone to my boss and said that I was not feeling empowered to handle a problem involving a peer operating in another country, he probably would have fired me on the spot. In his eyes, this would be akin to not doing anything while my boat was sinking because the hole was at the other end from where I was sitting, and no one empowered me to take action.

You do not wait for permission. You grab a bucket and start bailing.

In the end, there are people who do and there are people who don't do. *The world is run by people who do.* You have to choose which type of person to be.

SO WHY DON'T PEOPLE EMPOWER THEMSELVES?

Approximately two-thirds of the people responding to our At Work survey believe that they are "empowered" in their jobs. The remaining third say that they are not, or do not know if they are. The reality for this latter group is that they do not want to empower themselves.

There are three reasons why people do not want to empower themselves:

1. Some people do not know that they can empower themselves. It has never occurred to them. They may not have any role models who have shown them what empowerment looks like and what someone can accomplish through empowerment.
2. In some cases, people are reluctant to overstep their bounds. This is particularly true of people who work in functional organizations with rigid structures. These types of organizations may leave little opportunity for empowerment, or may actively discourage it.
3. Others may have tried to empower themselves in the past, only to be slapped down for their efforts.

Of these reasons, only the third one makes any sense to me. No true leader would cite the first two reasons for not empowering herself.

Many people are afraid or too weak to stand up and do what is right. They find it easier to blame others and complain about the system than to take action.

Empowerment is a choice that you are free to make. Keep in mind that your choice carries consequences for your career—present and future.

The Bottom Line

» The world is run by people who *do*. Grab a bucket.

Next Steps

1. Next time you have a problem getting something done, ask yourself what you would like to happen, then go about doing it.

2. When people tell you they are not empowered, ask them what it would take for them to empower themselves—and then become their mentor or coach in this area.

NINETEEN

Managing Your Boss

As a manager, you may think that your only job is to make sure your team and direct reports maximize their performance and achieve their objectives. You would be wrong — or, at least, you would be focusing only *on part* of what you need to do.

Managing is not limited to your team. Inevitably, you need to manage your peers and, more importantly, more senior managers and executives, *especially your boss*. In fact, managing your boss will have nearly as much impact on your performance as managing subordinates.

Think about it: you can have the best performing team with the highest morale and quality, and it will not mean much from a career perspective unless your boss is aware of that achievement and how you accomplished it.

In addition, there are bound to be times when you need your boss's help and influence to get something done. When those times come, you need to manage the situation and your boss to ensure that you get what you need.

How well you manage *up*wards largely determines the size of your next bonus, the timing of your next promotion, the content of your next role, and how the rest of the company perceives you.

The Challenge of Managing Upwards

Managing upwards can be hampered by lack of proximity and limited face time. These days, your boss may be across the hall or your boss could be in another building, another state, or even another country. In addition, most managers and executives, like you, are overextended. Managing upward is like delegating in reverse.

Given all of that, managing upwards becomes an exercise in making the most of the time and attention you do get from your boss. Chances are you get few opportunities to make sure that your boss knows what you are doing, and is engaged in your activities and those of your team.

Making the most of those opportunities involves learning to be proactive and letting your boss know the issues and challenges you face. It also means being prepared to take advantage of any time you do get with your boss whether in person or via telephone.

How to Manage Upwards

In one of my management positions, I made a lengthy presentation to my then-boss. At the end, I approached her to find out what she thought of the presentation and what I had said. While she made nice comments and said good things, it was clear to me she had so much on her mind that she had not really paid attention to anything I said.

This experience taught me the real importance of managing upwards. Most senior people are working on four or five complicated problems or issues that are unique and specific to each individual's role. Chances are good that you are not one of those four or five things. Moreover, given that those four or five things all tend to be bad problems, you don't want to be one of them.

Recognizing the limited mental bandwidth your boss has available for you is the first step in managing upwards effectively. Here are the other issues you should keep in mind:

1. Managing upwards is an exercise in managing expectations and then delivering on those expectations.

2. Your boss is unlikely to know how much good work you are doing if you don't tell him. Send a weekly or monthly report on how you are doing and ask for regular reviews so that you can explain that report.

3. Figure out the best way to give your boss enough information and input so that you can use her influence when you need it and get rewarded for what you accomplish. Do not make the mistake of overloading your already overloaded boss with information whenever you see or talk to her. Find out how your boss likes to get information and supply it that way. Just because you prefer long e-mails does not mean your boss does.

4. Focus your meetings with your boss on coming to an agreement on what needs to be done. From there, you can empower yourself to determine the best way to accomplish the resulting objectives.

5. Your boss also will not appreciate the obstacles you overcome unless he understands those obstacles and why they existed. Help him to understand the challenges you face and communicate metrics that gauge progress toward fixing those issues.

In my case, I recognized that my error was in providing my boss with *too much* information. The next time I had time with my boss, I took a different approach:

1. I identified the issues on which I needed her input.
2. I made her decision as easy as possible by conducting all of the work, analysis, and information-gathering before meeting with her.
3. Before meeting with my boss, I also discussed the issue and the proposed solution with my team and the other people involved. I wanted everyone on board with what I was proposing.
4. Rather than coming up with the answers so that she could just say "yes," I focused on what I thought we needed to do and the best options available to do that.
5. The final step was to present all of this information as succinctly as possible to make it easy for her to make the final decision.

By taking this approach, I helped my boss to do her job, rather than expecting her to do my job for me.

WHAT NOT TO DO

Problems with managing upwards start when communication becomes unbalanced. Communicating too much is sometimes worse than communicating too little. Don't be a pest.

It is appropriate to ask for advice and guidance, but doing so requires just as much preparation as presenting information. Be concise and focused in asking for what you need and in presenting data and analysis that will help your boss provide the necessary input. *Nothing will derail your career faster than asking for time with your boss and then looking like you do not know what you are doing.* Your boss may also think you are trying to hog too much of his bandwidth, and may start to avoid you until he starts planning work without you in mind.

This does not mean you should shy away from becoming a resource for your boss. You can become one by responding to questions quickly and accurately, taking on side projects, and working across teams well so your boss doesn't need to facilitate anything. Helping your boss to be successful adds a lot of goodwill.

You can also go too far. I have been in reviews where executives say that a potential candidate is "too focused on managing upwards." Making the boss happy is not more important than getting the work done. You should be careful not to be perceived as more focused on managing upwards than on managing your team.

THE BOTTOM LINE

» Managing your boss has almost as much impact on your performance and future career track than managing your subordinates.

NEXT STEPS

1. Write down as objectively and compactly as possible what you would like your boss to know about the performance or challenges of you and your team.

2. Review those points with your boss at your next review.

TWENTY

What to Do When You Get a New Boss

When a new boss comes on board, your first few meetings are very important. If you do not do your best to get off on the right foot with a new boss, you can find yourself on the sidelines. As they say, you only get one chance to make a good first impression.

When you first begin working with a new boss, how you talk to and work with your boss sets the tone for the rest of your relationship. If you make a mistake or offend your boss early on, you can derail your career.

During my career, I did make a poor first impression with a new boss. While that poor first impression did not trigger my eventual departure from the company, I do believe it was a contributing factor.

I have been the new boss myself a few times. I am always amazed by the interactions of people in their first meeting with me. Some people never take the meeting beyond the initial handshake and small talk. Others try to do too much and recite their resume to me within the first few minutes. These actions do not generate a positive impression.

The importance of establishing a solid foundation with the boss increases significantly as you take on more senior roles. A junior manager has many more options available if the relationship with a new boss does not click. However, senior managers, by definition, have fewer opportunities to move on. There are far fewer senior management positions than there are junior ones.

MAKING A GOOD FIRST IMPRESSION

Professionals with career aspirations need to know the four elements to establish a good working relationship with a new boss so as to avoid derailing their career within the company.

1. BE WELCOMING

Bosses are like anyone else starting a new job: they are nervous on their first day, even though they may not show it. Bosses do want to feel welcome. That does not mean you should "suck up" to the new boss. Just be as welcoming to the boss as you would want someone to be to you on your first day.

When you have an opportunity to approach the new boss, introduce yourself and tell the boss what your responsibilities are in the department. *This is a good time to offer your support for whatever the boss plans to do in his new role.*

This sounds simple, and it is. Yet this type of approach will be memorable. I always remembered people positively when they made it a point to approach me. Likewise, I remembered less favorably those whom I had to approach first. Some even appeared to be avoiding me. Although they were usually on business trips or stuck in long multiday meetings, they still could have made an effort. If I was not important enough for them to simply send a "Welcome!" e-mail, what did they think I would take from that?

I remember starting one job where one of the people who had wanted that job would be reporting to me. As an olive branch, I suggested he open my first town hall-style employee meeting and introduce me. My thinking was that this would help him reposition himself and save some face. Before the meeting, we agreed he would speak for five minutes and I would speak for fifteen minutes; this would be followed by ten minutes of question-taking so that we could wrap things up in half an hour.

When the time came, however, he spoke for twenty minutes, leaving me with just ten minutes for my presentation and any questions. Rather than make a fuss, I did my presentation in five minutes in order to leave another five minutes for questions. Everyone in the room recognized what the other person had done, and some even made comments to me about it later. Although I understood the man's actions, he lost an opportunity to look bigger than the situation. His misuse of the opportunity made him lose face.

2. BE OPEN AND TRANSPARENT

When she first arrives, a new boss assesses the department or the team, figuring out how things work and identifying problems and opportunities. When you have your first review with a new boss, be open and transparent about current business issues, both the good and the bad. Although everyone wants to emphasize the good news by telling it first, most new bosses will say that finding out about the bad news is more important.

When telling the new boss any bad news, be factual. You are giving the boss a "heads-up" on issues he may be facing. By stating the facts, you avoid being labeled as the "team gossip." Even if the boss would like to hear gossip and welcomes the information, he will not respect you for relaying it.

By sticking to the facts, you highlight your own capabilities. How you relay this information and what you relay convey a great deal about your ability to process and evaluate situations.

I still clearly recall how people approached me in my first few days on the job as a manager. Charlene was one of the first to introduce herself to me. During the course of our first few conversations, Charlene relayed some past experiences with the team, including productivity problems and their probable causes.

This information was invaluable to me as a new manager. The way in which Charlene discussed the information was extremely helpful. She spoke in specifics: where she thought the bottlenecks were (slow feedback from, and reluctant information-sharing by, other teams); solutions the last manager had tried; and why each had failed.

It was also a sign of things to come. Charlene wanted team performance to improve. She remained a strong resource for me during my tenure with that team. Collectively, we solved the problems and improved results. The experience also helped Charlene in her career. I gave her additional responsibility and she thrived. In fact, she left that team to take on a management role herself.

Of course, not all new bosses are willing to listen. Some may come in as if they already know all the answers, instead of taking the time to listen and understand the real situation. These "shoot-from-the-hip" bosses tend to come in with very clear views of what is right (not much) and what is wrong (a lot) with the team. Even if you tell this type of boss something that is an accurate reflection of the situation, you may simply be reinforcing in the new boss's mind that you may be part of the problem and not part of the proposed solution. The best way to protect yourself in this situation is to say nothing, then do all that you can to not run afoul of the new boss's preconceptions.

Before you say anything, assess whether the boss is a "listening boss" or a "shoot-from-the-hip boss." If you have a listening boss, your openness and transparency will serve you well. Ironically, in my experience, the bosses who talk about their great listening skills tend to be the ones least likely to listen to anyone.

You have heard the adage, "We have two ears and one mouth, and we should use them in that proportion." You will see in a short time if your new boss follows this rule.

3. BE HELPFUL

Coming into a new situation cold, a new boss does not always know whom to talk to or where to look for things. What he should do is read Michael Watkins's book, *The First 90 Days: Critical Success Strategies for New Leaders at All Levels.*

New bosses need to learn and understand quickly company processes—that is, the way things get done, and who does what.

If you offer help and guidance during a new boss's first few days and weeks, your boss may appreciate it very much. Moreover, your boss is apt to remember those who helped and those who just stood by and watched.

All bosses value people who help make them successful. You can help yourself by becoming a reliable resource to your boss.

4. BE MOTIVATED

The worst way to welcome a new boss is by looking like a manager who is struggling or adrift. Do not slack off just because there is a new boss. The boss may be new to the team or the company, but she is probably not new to management. Chances are good that your new boss knows when someone is not putting in a full effort.

In fact, a new boss will watch you carefully. Unless you know the boss well, you do not know how a manager defines and judges "slacking off." One of the best things you can do is watch the new boss's work ethic: what time does the boss come in? How late does the boss work? Does the boss handle e-mail on weekends and when traveling? How quickly does the boss expect people to respond to requests and actions?

While I do not think you need to copy the new boss's behavior, you do need to understand how the boss works. *The boss's behavior is your best insight into the boss's view of "full-time work" and how you should behave as his employee.*

Most new bosses judge the capabilities of their teams within the first ninety days in a new role. This often means assessing whom to change, whom to promote—and whom to let go. Those ninety days offer an opportunity to set a good example for the whole team by demonstrating your support and cooperation for the new boss. Show the boss how hungry you are for improvement.

Often, a new manager has the authority to promote and improve salaries as needed, particularly if the change is based on some trauma to the organization. If you can recognize this, then you may find an opportunity. But beware: if you misread the situation or the person, this move can have the opposite effect to what you want or expect. (More on this in the next chapter.)

144

THE BOTTOM LINE

» Welcome your new boss, be transparent and factual about your team and work experiences—and get back to work!

NEXT STEPS

1. Observe your boss's work ethic, and compare it to how you work.

2. At a future review, ask your boss about first impressions of the team, and what you could have done to be more helpful when the boss first arrived.

3. Read *The First 90 Days: Critical Success Strategies for New Leaders at All Levels* by Michael Watkins.

TWENTY-ONE

WHAT *NOT* TO SAY WHEN YOU GET A NEW BOSS

In Chapter 20, we talked about developing a positive relationship with a new boss to avoid being seen as a Stuck-in-the-Middle Manager who lacks drive and vision. *You must avoid the common mistakes people make when they meet a new boss for the first time.*

Saying the wrong thing to a new boss is easier to do than you may realize. Even after years of advising others about this, I still make these mistakes from time to time. People become so accustomed to communicating in a certain way that they forget or do not realize how their words can be misconstrued by an outsider or a newcomer. Moreover, something that everyone around you accepts as the "way it is" may, to a new set of ears, sound defensive or arrogant.

When I joined a new company in a senior management position, a member of my team immediately told me that he did not think the company would survive much longer. He continued with a lot more negative imagery: the company was going "down the drain," "up in flames," and so on. In essence, he told me that I had made a dumb move by joining the company.

In reality, the company was doing better than he gave it credit for. He was just someone who was frustrated in his job and looking for a way to vent. However, my first meeting with him left me feeling negative about him. I wondered if he was "recoverable." Did he have the potential to be a productive team member? In the end, his perspective worked against him. He left the team and the company shortly afterwards.

In my years in management, I have identified the five worst things you can say to a new boss. I have experienced all of them as a boss, and I have had the misfortune of saying a few of them myself.

1. NEVER START BY SAYING YOU "SHOULD ALREADY HAVE BEEN PROMOTED!"

It never ceases to amaze me how many people do this and think it is a good strategy. Managers are not favorably impressed when, in a first meeting, they are told that their predecessor had promised this individual a promotion, and that it was years late, and...and...and....

Personally, I have never promoted anyone who did this. I have never even considered it. If I talked to my peers about it, I rarely heard anything that supported a future promotion for that individual. Instead, the feedback is that the person has an "unrealistic view" of her skills and contributions. A reason exists for why she did not get the promotion—and that reason will exist for the new boss just as surely as it did for the old boss.

If you are the new boss, you have to consider whether the old boss recognized that the team member was never going to get promoted, and what the old boss did about it. If the old boss told the team member that a promotion would not be forthcoming and the team member simply chose not to hear, that signals that you may experience problems with the team member. Your Human Resources team should know the answer to what the old boss told the team member.

If the old boss did not tell the team member because he did not have time or was too enmeshed in his own stalled-out career or issues to have that difficult conversation, then you have other problems. If Stuck-in-the-Middle Management was pervasive, other team members also may not have received honest evaluations of their career prospects.

If your new boss brings up the idea of your promotion with you during an early meeting, that is another situation entirely. *Listen carefully but still do not push for a promotion. Simply say that you are looking for opportunities to "prove yourself."*

2. NEVER EXPRESS DOUBT ABOUT
THE VALUE OF THE TEAM'S WORK OR MEMBERS

You may think doing so is clever or funny. It isn't. Devaluing the work by the team or its members is never a good idea. By saying such things, you indirectly devalue your new boss. You convey the idea that the new boss is working in a division or as head of a team that no one respects or cares about. That is not very smart.

Unbeknownst to you, the new boss may have been brought in to make changes and improvements. Focus the conversation on potential process improvements and other changes that can help the team.

3. NEVER BE RUDE WHEN MENTIONING YOUR LAST BOSS

If you badmouth your old boss to the new boss, your actions reflect badly on *you*. If you are willing to say bad things about the old boss, what is to stop you from saying bad things about the new boss at some point?

You may not know why your old boss left. The reasons may be far more complex than you think. You may know only part of the story. Moreover, the new boss may know the old boss well. They could be personal friends, or the new boss could consider the old boss to be a mentor.

You do not know what information the old boss and the new boss are sharing. If you focus too much on the negative, the new boss could consider you to be too negative in general, and perhaps part of the problem.

Avoid discussions of senior management skills, office politics, and speculation until you get to know the new boss better. You do not want to be known as a "boss hater" by the new management.

4. NEVER BLAME THE COMPETITION
OR THE MARKET FOR ANY WORK PROBLEMS

Few things are more off-putting than someone who blames his problems on other people or circumstances. I have worked with enough new people to recognize that many have a tendency to do just that in an off-handed way. Even if some truth exists to what you say, the words can still have a negative effect on your new boss.

I made this mistake with a new boss when I tried to make a point that a competitor used its market power to lock our company out of an opportunity. To this day, I know I was right about what I said. However, I also know that he believed I was making an excuse for my team's failure to execute. In many ways, he was right. Blaming others for your own faults (or your team's fault) is one of the hallmarks of a Stuck-in-the-Middle Manager.

When bosses are new to a company or a role, they tend to approach things with a more open mind. Their mandate as the new boss is to succeed where others have not by bringing creative thinking and new approaches to the role.

The company chose the new boss for several reasons. The boss may have a better network and more relevant experiences. To the new boss—assuming he does not practice Stuck-in-the-Middle Management—anything is possible in his new role. He sees no limits to his success. In this context, the new boss will take any comments you make about competitors as a sign of your inability to find ways around those competitors, and consider your issues with the market insular.

Instead of focusing on negatives, focus on what you do and what you bring to the company.

5. NEVER, EVER COMPLAIN ABOUT
THE COMPANY TO A NEW BOSS

In the same way you should not blame the competition or the market, *do not badmouth the company and its prospects — especially in your first encounters with a new boss.* New bosses believe that they can do something to make things better. They do not want to hear that there is no hope and that they should give up.

You may not know the scope the new leader has to make changes and innovate. Therefore, your comments may be out of context with what the new boss wants, needs, and can do. While such remarks may cause no immediate harm, they do not make you look like a long-term player for the team.

If you think something really is wrong in the company or on the team, the boss needs to know that at some point. First, though, establish a relationship with the boss in order to establish your own credibility before broaching these types of subjects.

THE BOTTOM LINE

» Focus on what you can do and what you bring to the company—rather than on any negatives about your company or team—when first meeting your new boss.

NEXT STEPS

1. In the initial meeting with a new boss, always identify and note the best things about your job and department.

2. A new boss brings opportunity—so consider any restrictions on your team's execution capabilities and ask how they might be improved or lifted.

3. Make sure you establish a good positive and open relationship with the new boss from day one.

TWENTY-TWO

FINDING LEVERAGE TO
GET THINGS DONE

As a middle manager, one of your greatest challenges is *convincing someone to take action when you do not have the power to compel them to action.* In the next two chapters we will look at power and influence. While they often feel like and look like the same thing, in the workplace they are not.

Power is typically something you either have or are given. *Influence* is something that you need to use, typically when you do not have power.

First, let's review power. Everyone has some level of power no matter what one's position in a company. But let's face it: only the CEO and a few select others have the power to compel someone to take action no matter what the situation. The rest of us have to use what leverage we can find to influence people toward action and to support our ideas.

Achieving anything worthwhile requires the ability to find leverage to move a more powerful force. Simply pushing against a powerful force wastes time and energy.

Early in my career, I dealt with a vice president many levels above me. This executive was proposing a solution that I thought was wrong, and I wanted to convince him to consider an alternative solution.

He had far more power than I did. Therefore, I could not hope to compel him to change his approach.

We also were not peers. If I simply disengaged from him, nothing would happen, and he would simply continue on his chosen path.

The challenge for me was to find a way to influence that executive when I had no power to do so.

I decided to approach the executive during a quiet time and explain why I thought his chosen solution would not work. I provided data to back up my assertions and proposed an alternative solution that I had developed. I also suggested that he seek input on the viability of both potential solutions from other members of the team.

In this case, the result was mixed. The executive did not abandon his chosen solution, but he did modify it to address some of the weaknesses I had pointed out. In retrospect, it may have been the best outcome I could have hoped for.

GAINING LEVERAGE

If you want to accomplish something in an organization, you must be able to convince people of the merits of your ideas while making the case that supporting your ideas is to their benefit. Unfortunately, having the best idea in the room is not enough in most cases.

How can you gain that necessary leverage?

Sometimes in the corporate world, it all comes down to power. How much power you and the other person have relative to each other will guide your interactions and choices as you seek to influence them.

Let's look at three potential scenarios that show different approaches to influencing someone based on the relative level of power between the two people.

SCENARIO #1:

YOU HAVE MORE POWER THAN

THE PERSON YOU NEED TO INFLUENCE.

Having more power than the person you need to influence gives you the upper hand. If we were to consider this scenario in terms of physical power with the objective to get someone to leave the room, you could use your additional power to "push" that person out of the room.

In some cases, this type of "pushing" could take the form of a threatened punitive action or punishment to motivate someone to do what you want.

There are significant implications to taking that approach, many of them negative. Your actions could adversely affect your working relationship with the other person. Your actions could adversely affect that person's motivation and productivity. Even if such actions achieve your immediate objective of action, it is less clear that the other person will continue to do what you want.

However, this "pushing" could also take a more positive form, and have positive implications for the working relationship. For example, you could order someone to do something, and then provide some sort of reward, such as a strong performance review, pay raise, or more responsibility.

SCENARIO #2:

YOU HAVE LESS POWER THAN THE PERSON

YOU NEED TO INFLUENCE.

Let's continue with the scenario in which you need to convince someone to leave the room, but with one change: you now have less power than the person you are trying to remove from the room. As a result, you either need to pull that person out of the room by force, or (more likely) persuade that person to leave the room.

In a real-life corporate scenario, this means convincing the individual that it is in his best interest to leave the room. This scenario requires strong influencing skills (discussed in Chapter 23) that must be honed over time.

My interactions with the vice president I mentioned earlier fit this scenario. I could not compel the vice president to take action, so I convinced him it was in his best interest to consider and to implement my ideas. I emphasized how my solution would benefit the company (and, by extension, the vice president) by increasing sales in one product line by a full percentage point more than the vice president's solution. To substantiate my point, I used sales data to show where the increases would come from.

Some might argue that in this situation, you should try to assert power even if you do not have it. I have seen it argued that you should always try to be the "alpha" in any situation by never backing down and never showing any weakness. While that may well work in *Fight Club*, it typically does not play well at work.

People with real power over you need to know you respect that power. If you do not show that respect, then you will hear phrases like, "She doesn't know how to read an organization chart." In other words—you do not know your station, or understand your level of importance at work, which is something that can derail your career.

That does not mean you should always walk away and surrender.

One of the first lessons I learned when I started to work with very senior executives was that it's sometimes better to look responsive than smart! At some point, it was better to say that I would go "work on something and come back with a good answer fast." At that point in my career, the senior executives in my company valued my responsiveness over my proving I knew something they did not.

I had "learned to read the organization chart."

SCENARIO #3:

YOU BOTH HAVE EQUAL AMOUNTS OF POWER.

When you need to influence someone with the same amount of power, it is easy for the situation to escalate into a power struggle. Rather than working together to identify the best available solution, both parties dig in and champion their own ideas above all others with little room for negotiation and compromise.

We all get stuck in the middle of these sorts of situations. In my career, I have struggled to convince certain colleagues of what I considered to be the right answer until the discussion became a shouting match.

In these situations, typically there are no right answers; there are only opinions. As tempers heat and words fly, it becomes difficult to get to any resolution. While open and loud communication can have a cathartic feeling to it, it often creates a situation in which it is impossible to resolve the problem because you are angry and shouting.

The simplest way to deal with scenarios like these is to *disengage and walk away*. At some point, either you or the other party should have to leave the room of their own volition.

In a business situation, this approach leaves you free to fight another day. Tempers simmer down, and you can try again while keeping emotions out of the situation. At this point, you have a better opportunity to build a bridge between you and the other person so that you can develop a common solution to the problem.

If you work in an organization where the people are passionate about what they do, and open and loud communication is the norm, then do not be surprised when people raise their voices from time to time. I would even argue that these discussions can be healthy as long as the communication is open and the par ties involved look to resolve the differences and compromise in the end. I would much rather work in that type of environment than one that is passive-aggressive and people hide their feelings and motives.

We will talk more about passive-aggressive behavior in Chapter 35.

The Bottom Line

» Learning how to deal with varying levels of power and how to convince people to support your positions will pay enormous dividends throughout your career.

NEXT STEPS

1. Consider the people you work with and your relative level of power compared to them.

2. Identify and practice various scenarios in which you find leverage to convince those individuals to support your ideas.

TWENTY-THREE

INFLUENCING DIFFERENT TYPES OF PEOPLE

In Chapter 22, we discussed the difference between power and influence. While power may be given, influence is something you need to take or make for yourself. No one will give it to you.

Twenty-First Century Executives must be able to influence and convince others to take action. Those who cannot impact and persuade others often become Stuck-in-the-Middle Managers.

Influencing people is an especially important skill in the age of the cross-functional team. If you are part of such a team or simply need a peer to take action or support an initiative, you must understand that people always need a *good reason* to act.

I want to emphasize one important ground rule: it is very difficult, not to mention unethical, to influence colleagues into doing something they really should not be doing or that is not in their best interest.

Instead, it is best to *focus the powers of your influence on getting people to do the right things.* In most business situations, this means motivating someone to do something that makes sense when there is no obvious reason for action. Salespeople are particularly good at this because the power of influence is crucial to their success. The power of influence is vital for overall success.

Laura, a finance manager charged with implementing a more streamlined accounts payable process, had to convince her peers in other departments and functional areas to support changes for submitting invoices. Laura recognized the critical importance of the changes. Laura also realized that other people needed to understand and comply with the new process.

Just before introducing the new process, Laura sent out a lengthy e-mail explaining the changes and the new electronic invoice submission process. When the implementation began, only a third of those managers who received the e-mail submitted their invoices electronically. The rest kept doing things the way they always had.

WHAT WAS THE PROBLEM?

Laura sent out an impersonal e-mail. She made no attempt to customize her approach to the people she sought to influence. Few did respond and adopted the new process; most chose to ignore it. Some may have worried that the changes would cause them more work. If the new electronic invoice submission process was to succeed, Laura needed to find the right way to approach and influence those managers who were not complying.

UNDERSTAND BEFORE YOU INFLUENCE

Laura is not alone in this struggle to influence people. We all face it, some of us on a daily basis. The key is to adapt our influencing style to the needs and preferences of the person whom we seek to influence.

One effective model is based on the work of R.W. Wallen, who identified three types of executive personalities. Charles

Handy then summarized these models in a book, *Understanding Organizations.*

In general, Handy's model suggested that you are likely to be dealing with one of three types of people:

1. Logical people. These are people who carefully read the manual when they buy a new gadget and follow the steps to using it. Logical people follow rules and will not think "out of the box" even though you want them to. To influence this type of person, you need to emphasize the logic and reasoning behind what you are trying to do. Lay out your point in sequence, and focus on the reasons for your ideas and their benefits. Someone logical (type #1) may have gotten Laura's e-mail and not understood all the reasons for the changes. This type will not implement something that does not make logical sense.

2. People people. These folks focus on relationships and inter-personal communication. When they get a new gadget, they ask for help from others who have the same or similar gadget. With these people, you typically have to take the time to get to know them. Rather than relying solely on logic, they want to discuss a subject, usually over lunch or coffee, so that they can explore every angle. A people person may have been offended by Laura's impersonal approach or may have assumed that the invoicing change was not an important issue. They think that if it was important, Laura would have called them, or even come by to see them.

3. Net-net people. When net-net people get a new gadget, they just plug it in and see what happens. They don't want to see how you got the answer. They just want to know what the answer is. These people want to get to the point quickly; they want the net-net. Many senior executives fall into this category. This doesn't mean you don't have to have logic or reasons behind your ideas. Net-net people will certainly ask for that information if they need it. Just don't make the mistake of spending too long getting to your point. When the net-net people got Laura's e-mail, they probably did not even read it. They got to the third sentence, at which point Laura had not asked them to do anything, and they deleted the rest of the e-mail. "Oh," they say, "I didn't see any action for me to take in the e-mail."

UNDERSTANDING IS RELATIVE

Your ability to influence others depends on how well you understand yourself and your own style, and how your style impacts the people you are trying to influence. You need to influence using the style that works for them, not just for you.

On this scale, most people think of me as a net-net person (just think how many of these chapters have three simple ideas contained in a few paragraphs rather than long pages of prose). But a few years ago, I had a challenging time influencing a customer. The customer I was trying to influence was very much a logical person.

I kept trying to get to the bottom line. He kept asking me to explain why. As a result of the difference in our personal styles and preferences, I found this customer rather frustrating and difficult to work with. By contrast, a colleague who, as an engineer, was also a logical person, found that customer to be very approachable and insightful. My problem was that I expected the customer to think like I did. I wanted him to be like me in the model.

There is clearly no right or wrong place to be in the model. No good manager or executive is better because she is one of these types over the other. In fact, we have a little bit of all of them in us. I was taught the model while enrolled in a course in the UK and, while I do not remember the company that ran the course,

I still have a book by some of the instructors called *First Find Your Hilltop.*[1]

As they taught the model, we are all made up of a triangle of these styles, with one style at each corner. The trick to using the model is not where you place yourself within the triangle—something you should try to do—but where you are relative to the person you are trying to influence. *Then notice the difference between the two of you.*

INFLUENCING
DIFFERENT TYPES OF PEOPLE

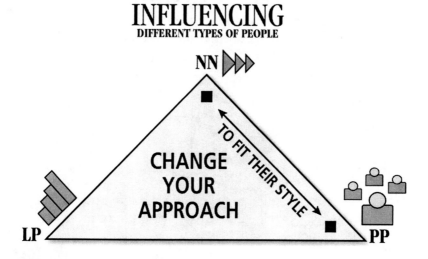

What you realize is *that you need to adjust your approach and expectations to these differences when it comes to influencing someone.* If I am working with a logical person, I know to go into that meeting with a solid, logical business case for what I want to do. If I am working with a people person, I set aside time to meet for coffee or lunch to discuss things. When I meet with people who are net-net, well, let's say, these are very short meetings.

---

1. Originally published by Hutchinson Business Books in 1990. ISBN-10: 0091744059

As you learn to adjust your style to match the needs of the person you are dealing with, you will see your influence grow over time.

THE BOTTOM LINE

» It matters how the people you are trying to influence want to receive information. You need to adapt your style to them.

NEXT STEPS

1. When you meet with people, assess how their influencing style compares to yours. Plot them on the triangle compared to you.

2. During a meeting, start to adjust your style to more closely match that person's style and see what happens.

3. Think about one person you are having difficulty influencing. In which category does he fit compared to you? Now, build a plan to influence him using his personality type, not yours.

TWENTY-FOUR

ESCALATING: TAKING THINGS TO THE HIGHER-UPS

Unless you work in a perfect company or organization, someday someone will make a decision or will plan to take action that is bad for your company. As a 21st Century Executive with integrity, you reject the type of stick-your-head-in-the-sand-ostrich behavior that would allow you to ignore this situation. So, the question becomes, *What can you do about it?*

While you might think the answer is obvious, I have watched many people go to great lengths to avoid escalating a bad situation. I even saw a note from one manager to another with pages of reasons why a decision was bad that concluded with the line, "But I am not escalating the situation." My question to the manager was, "Why not?"

Early in my career, one of my bosses gave me solid advice concerning my responsibility to escalate issues by bringing them to the attention of someone higher in the organization when necessary. At the time, I had an issue with a decision one of my peers had made, but I was reluctant to say anything negative about it.

Not surprisingly, my boss disagreed with my approach. He told me, "If you think someone is basing a decision on bad data or insufficient data, you have a responsibility to escalate that issue to someone higher in the organization for the good of the company." My boss also warned that the decision to escalate should never be personal, but always based on sound data and business sense.

This is good advice that I have relied on several times in my career. *Escalation* can be a net positive for your company and for you when you do it well and for the right reasons.

THE ART OF ESCALATING

To escalate the right way and for the right reasons, you need to be able to answer three questions: why should I escalate, how should I escalate, and what are the downsides?

1. WHY SHOULD YOU ESCALATE?

Although you do not want to escalate every situation, people do not escalate as often as they should in my experience. When Stuck-in-the-Middle Managers rule the company, people often view escalation as negative or confrontational. Effective escalation is neither. The decision to escalate should not be a difficult one if you have done the right things first.

Steve, one of my peers back when I was a manager, felt it necessary to escalate a manufacturing process design decision another manager had made. The decision was designed to streamline a specific process to make it less costly and more efficient. Steve's main concern was that this manager had only considered performance data from about half of the company's manufacturing plants. Without data from the other half, the expectations for the cost effectiveness and efficiency of the process change might not be as significant. When Steve approached the decision maker with the data and evidence, that individual chose not to listen to his arguments.

Steve's decision to escalate was the right one for the following reasons:

- He focused on the decision itself and not the particular person who made the decision. In other words, *he escalated the decision on its own merits.*
- His goal was to make sure that the decision was the right one for the company and based on all relevant and available input and data.
- He didn't choose to escalate simply because he disagreed with the process used to make the decision. His concerns focused on the fact that the data and input behind the decision were lacking and that the analysis was incorrect or based on the wrong assumptions.
- He didn't focus on the manager's judgment but on the data the manager used to make his decision.
- Before escalating, Steve had gone to the manager to have a conversation to resolve the issue. He did not try to avoid a possible confrontation by sending an e-mail.
- By escalating, Steve had a specific goal in mind: to introduce new input, data, and analysis that could make a significant difference to the final outcome.

When you escalate based on these criteria, a good management team will respect your request and be ready to lend support while assisting with the effort.

By going through these steps, you also start to build the documentation and evidence needed to support your case.

2. How to escalate

Once you decide to escalate, you must first tell the other party why you disagree with his decision and analysis. At this point, you should try to resolve the situation between the two of you or ask a colleague to mediate the situation before going any further. This is always better done face-to-face or over the phone if you are not local.

One of the worst ways you can do this is by e-mail. We talked about the challenges of e-mail in Chapter 13, and how e-mail can be misinterpreted. This is particularly true when you challenge someone on a decision he has made.

Carefully listen to the arguments of the person to whom you are talking. You cannot expect people to listen to you if you are not willing to listen to them. If your objective is just to get the other person to say, "I'm wrong," you will fail. The best result from this type of conversation is that the other side will modify rather than change his opinion and decision.

If that individual refuses to change the decision or you are not convinced by the explanation, you need to say what you will do next, including to whom you plan to escalate the situation further.

Assuming the person who said "no" actually never had the power to say "yes" anyway, you can choose the person to whom you will escalate. *Follow the organizational chart.* While it may seem more efficient to escalate to the seniormost person, doing so is likely to alienate the people you bypass. Not everyone you escalate to has the ability to overturn the decision. You need to keep escalating until you find the person who can say yes to you and change the decision based on what you present. If that person still says no, that is when the escalation process ends.

Getting the escalating process right for yourself is important; helping someone else get this right may be even more crucial. As a manager, you may find yourself in a position where you need to talk someone on your team through the issues involved in how to escalate. Make sure you let your team know that you are willing to help and coach them through these sorts of actions. If your team members know you will support them, they are not only more likely to want to do the right thing, but also more likely to let you support them.

If someone on your team handles an escalation badly, take the time to coach that person on what she could do better next time. You can offer to be part of the escalation, but do not take over the process or manage things for the team. *It is important for everyone to develop these skills.* If you do too much, your team may not want to try escalating in the future.

3. WHAT CAN GO WRONG?

Escalations inevitably touch people's emotions and can therefore go wrong for many reasons. The best example is when someone escalates because of a perceived personal grudge or out of a desire to prove someone wrong rather than for a legitimate business reason.

Escalation also becomes problematic when people focus on problems with the method or procedure rather than the outcome. You should not escalate just because someone comes to a decision using a method that differs from yours. If the decision is a sound one, the path the person took to get there is irrelevant.

It is also a good idea to avoid using your data to make your point for escalation. If you are going to escalate, base your argument on company-accepted data.

Finally, try to avoid escalating a decision that is representative of larger management or organizational issues. Escalation is not the best way to deal with those issues. For example, escalating a decision because a manager cannot cope with conflict or plays favorites will only reflect badly on you. You need to find other, more appropriate ways to deal with those problems. If you do not know if you have one of these larger issues, talk to your manager. They typically have a broader view of what is going on around you.

THE BOTTOM LINE

» Make sure any decision to escalate is about what is best for the business and the company, not what is best for you.

NEXT STEPS

1. Consider the last time you escalated something and did not get the result you wanted. Now review the steps cited in this chapter and identify what you missed.

2. Next time you have an issue to escalate, force yourself to go through the steps cited in this chapter. Watch the impact each step has.

3. In your team, discuss who has successfully escalated something, and what problems others have had when escalating.

SECTION III

MANAGING YOUR TEAM

THE ART OF
DELEGATING

See more about The Art of Delegating in Chapter 30.

TWENTY-FIVE

UNDERSTANDING THE DIFFERENCE BETWEEN MANAGEMENT AND LEADERSHIP

At some point in your 21st Century Executive career, you may find your role shifting from management to leadership. When I moved up to my first role as a director, I experienced a significant shift, not only in what was expected of me, but in how people interacted with me. I was no longer just a manager. I had become a *leader*.

Not many people are told that this perception shift is coming. Even fewer are given any training on what it means. Maybe that is why in our At Work survey, only 40 percent of the respondents saw their manager as a leader and more than just their manager. So, what's the difference between a manager and a leader?

To people who stall out in their careers, there is no difference between the two. If you aspire to more than Stuck-in-the-Middle Management, you will see important distinctions between management and leadership.

WHAT IS LEADERSHIP?

In the simplest definition, *managers* bring people together to accomplish agreed-upon and approved goals. A manager helps the more senior management and executives divide work into more manageable chunks and makes sure work is completed on time and to the right quality. First-line managers have only line employees reporting to them. Second-line managers have other managers reporting to them.

If you are a second-line manager or director, there is an expectation *that you will act less like a manager and more like a leader. Leaders* affect cultures and behaviors, and influence the people around them in order to accomplish a mission and to set and achieve goals.

The distinctions you will experience as you move from management to leadership are profound. It is unlikely that anyone will signal to you that it is now time to be a leader. I doubt that your boss is going to say, "Well done, you are now a leader."

If you take on a second-line management or director-level position and do not change your approach toward leadership, you are likely to hear about it during your next review. Your boss did not promote you so that you could practice outdated and stale thinking. Therefore, you may hear, "Okay, now it's your time to be a leader."

Once you decide to become a leader and start acting like one, the people below you will see you in a different light. When I first became a leader, I realized people looked to me for guidance, and not just to help the team achieve its goals. The team took everything I said much more seriously than they ever had when I was a manager.

Another difference is the authority that comes with taking a leadership position. First, you can be more successful at influencing people to do things just by asserting yourself as a leader. Even though you probably do not have the power to make people support you, good leadership is often so infectious that people want to follow you. Second, as a leader, you are going to be seen as part of the structure and heart of the company. I often tell new directors that they just became "the man" and are no longer part of "the system." They may not like it, but that's how they will be perceived.

When I chose to be a leader, I saw that the people above me expected more from me—but so did the people that reported to me. I was no longer simply implementing someone else's directives—I was setting those directives. More importantly, *I held responsibility for selling my ideas to others and influencing the overall direction of the enterprise.*

THREE BEHAVIORS OF LEADERS

Adjusting to a new leadership role takes time. When I first became a director, a more senior colleague warned me of the subtle and not-so-subtle changes I would experience as a newly minted leader. It wasn't until I was in the role of director and trying to get things done that the full significance of the change hit me.

Understanding how your role as a leader is different eases the transition. As I have watched managers transform into leaders over the years, I have seen three distinct sets of behaviors among those who made the best transition.

1. RECOGNIZE YOUR NEW POSITION

The cliché is that with great power comes great responsibility. So what you say and how you say it is critical. As a leader, you can no longer get away with some of the things you did as a manager, and definitely not the things you did as a frontline employee. You cannot be a leader and also be one of the guys/

girls in the office. Trying to fill both of those roles is a recipe for a Stuck-in-the-Middle Manager.

In his book, *Monday Morning Leadership*, David Cottrell highlights the key difference as you move from management to leadership: "You are no longer a passenger; you have become the driver… you lose some of the rights or freedoms you may have enjoyed in the past." *Drivers need to keep their eyes on the road and they need to know where they are going. If you get off-course, you need to find your way back to the right road.*

A good example of this transition is the way you do or don't engage in gossip. While we all know gossip is a bad thing and can do damage and harm, most of us find it hard to resist telling someone some inside scoop. We probably don't even think of it as gossip, but as sharing information with peers and colleagues. Gossiping amongst peers is one thing. Gossiping with your team when you are its leader takes on a very different meaning. If you are "the man" and you s ay something, then "the man" said something. Your gossip could be perceived as guidance — or even a preannouncement!

At the core of leadership is being worthy of trust and getting your people to trust in their leaders. In the At Work, 84 percent of those who believe they work for a leader — and not just a manager — said that they trust that leader. Just over half (51 percent) who work for a manager and not a leader say they either did not trust that manager or were not sure if they could trust that manager.

The simplest rule is to *never gossip*. Realistically, it is challenging to build relationships without some sharing. So here's what I do. I never gossip with people who are not at my level. I never gossip about something I know about. I tell people, "This is what I think, but I never gossip about things I know for sure!"

2. DEVELOP NEW AND DIFFERENT RELATIONSHIPS

The new set of responsibilities and expectations you take on as a leader resets your interpersonal relationships on the job. There is a different perception of what you say when you are in a leadership position. Weigh your words more carefully. When you do speak, your words have more gravity and impact because you are a leader.

As a leader, you also need to show that you understand what needs to be accomplished and the best way to do so. If you can demonstrate that you "get it," your teams will "get it" as well. If you show that you cannot be trusted or that you are uncertain in your decision-making (two true signs of Stuck-in-the-Middle Managers), it will be difficult to earn the trust and confidence of the people above or below you.

In my early days as a director, one of the most difficult changes was in my interpersonal relationships. People still expected me to act like I did when I was a manager. However, as a leader, I needed to keep a certain amount of distance. The most obvious example for me was in my social interactions. Rather than going out for an evening of drinking with my team, I would plan to show up to have just one drink with them, and then leave. If I wanted to socialize with people at work, I did it at my level or above. While this may appear to be "snobbish," there are important reasons for doing this.

Today, as a leader, I strive to have great managers and team leaders doing the work of management for me. Someone else watches over the day-to-day goal achievement. My biggest contributions are to set overall direction and empower the team by removing obstacles that might prevent them from achieving their goals. Given that many, if not most, of those obstacles come from relationships and conflicts with other teams, being on good terms with the leaders of those teams is critical. People like to work with people they like. That requires some social effort and building new relationships among leaders.

As you become a leader and move up in your organization, be aware that your relationships need to change for many reasons. Avoiding any chance of a sexual harassment accusation is one of them. Do not put yourself in a situation that might become difficult. If you become concerned that a situation is getting out of hand, extract yourself as soon as possible.

In most business cultures, drinking is not proof of leadership. I suggest a two-drink maximum and an early night. I have seen people at very senior levels break this rule. They have often lived to regret it. This may seem unfair, but, as with the rise of the designated driver, the rules have changed.

3. DEVELOP YOUR LEADERSHIP PHILOSOPHY

When most people move into a director role, they expect their job to be focused on managing people. But directors and all 21st Century Executives have a different mentality from that of managers—and that requires a leadership philosophy.

A *leadership philosophy* not only acts as a guide as you develop your leadership skills, but also provides your teams with the consistency necessary to maximize their effectiveness. Few things are more frustrating for your team than ever-changing feedback as to what approach you want them to take.

In Chapter 1, we talked about the importance of setting a destination for your career. I have found that the most critical element in leadership is *being able to define and communicate a vision of where you and your team are going.* In fact, it is the heart of my leadership philosophy. Not knowing where you are going is a good way to create and encourage lack of vision, initiative, and ownership among your teams and team members.

When I join a new team, I always share with them my philosophy and approach. It is sprinkled through the whole of the *3 Minute Mentor* website and this book.

I developed my approach by listening to the people around me, and from learning from those who influenced me. As you assume a leadership role, you must do the same.

THE BOTTOM LINE

» To be a leader, you must be able to define and communicate a vision of where you and your team are going.

NEXT STEPS

1. Ask yourself if you have really accepted the role of leader and, if so, what that means to you.

2. Look at your relationships, both the ones you have and the ones you need. Are these the right ones to help you lead your team?

3. Have you defined your leadership philosophy? If not, it is time to do so. Then go ahead and communicate it, in many ways, details, and actions, every workday.

TWENTY-SIX

THE PARADOX OF LEADERSHIP

Leaders have to deal with many difficult situations. Often, those situations are complicated and confusing. Leaders also need to be comfortable with the idea of a *paradox* — holding two conflicting thoughts at the same time. If you cannot do that, you are at risk of falling backwards into Stuck-in-the-Middle Management, compromising your career as a leader.

The first time I encountered a paradox as a manager, I was working on a project with a firm deadline and a limited budget. I learned that some of the key engineering and production people I needed to complete the project would not be available at any point during my project timeframe. Moreover, my limited budget did not allow me to bring in outside resources and experts.

I went to my boss and explained the situation. She heard me out and then told me in no uncertain terms that I still had to deliver the project.

I was flummoxed. I had no idea what to do. How could I complete this project when I had no one with engineering expertise on my team, there would be no one with engineering expertise in the company available to work on the project, and I had no budget to hire a consulting engineer?

I was facing a paradox, and somehow I knew that how well I managed the situation would have a tremendous impact on my career.

WHAT IS THE PARADOX OF LEADERSHIP?

A *paradox* is a statement that leads to a contradiction that defies logic, but is nevertheless true.

Joseph Heller created the most famous of all paradoxes in his book *Catch-22*. A *Catch-22 situation* occurs when someone is in need of something that can only be had by not needing it. Another paradox (one of my personal favorites) is sometimes known as the "lottery paradox." We all know that there is only one winning set of numbers in a large lottery. The paradox is that it is reasonable to believe that your lottery ticket is not the winner because the odds are so high. However, it is not reasonable to believe that no lottery ticket will win. Or to put it another way, the odds of winning are not greatly reduced by not buying a ticket!

As a business leader, you are most likely to encounter the leadership paradox when it comes to *resources*. People need more money (or people or time) to complete a project, but there is none to spare.

A paradox cannot be fixed. It is a fact of life. You must be prepared to manage and deal with a paradox when it arises. Unfortunately, you can get so caught up in the problem that you become paralyzed with indecision.

Instead of becoming paralyzed, *concentrate on finding ways to eliminate those things that constrain your abilities to act, manage the situation, and be effective.* The key is to focus on how to do things differently given the current situation and requirements.

Leaders do not hide behind excuses. Leaders have to find a way to achieve their goals regardless of the circumstances. The best leaders do not allow anything to limit their effectiveness.

Preparing to Deal with a Paradox

By the time you assume the type of leadership position in which paradoxes arise, you should have all of the tools necessary to deal with the situation. Managing a paradox is a key part of having the right approach (as discussed in Chapter 4). It requires a strong understanding of necessary trade-offs, strong problem- solving skills, and the ability to troubleshoot. If you aspire to leadership, you will need to acquire these types of skills and demonstrate effectiveness in using them.

You have to manage more than your own reaction to a paradox. When a paradox exists, members of your team could become paralyzed by the circumstances and look to blame others. Unless you manage the paradox effectively, your team is likely to halt work and start pointing fingers for the breakdown. As a manager or 21st Century Executive, you need to coach your team in accepting the existence of paradoxes, and to assure them help in dealing with them.

Managing a Paradox

The first step in managing a paradox is realizing and accepting that you can never get rid of all resource constraints. As long as businesses are trying to make money, business leaders will have to find ways to get things done with understaffed, underfunded projects and teams.

Next, you need to accept that part of leadership is pushing yourself and others *to do more with less.*

Paradoxes always exist. They cannot be fixed or removed. The only variable is *how well you manage them.*

When I faced my first paradox as a manager, I focused on calming myself down and helping my team recognize that we still had to complete our objectives and our project. Once the team understood that I was prepared to work around our paradox, they were more relaxed and willing to work through the challenges.

Something had to change about how and what we were to deliver. Therefore, the next step for us was to go back to all the assumptions we had made about the project so that we could reconsider the project plan, design, and any other variables in light of the paradox. (Bear in mind it can be hard for some people to recognize elements that they view as fixed are, in fact, variable, but this needs to be done.)

In the end, we compromised on some of our original design specifications. When we went back to the customer for the project to discuss these changes, the customer not only agreed with the changes but also made other helpful recommendations. These changes allowed us to refocus and deliver a working solution on budget. Although the project was completed later than planned, it was still within the customer's acceptable window.

The secret of paradoxes is that *you have to manage through them.* Your team probably does so instinctively every day. It is only the truly challenging ones that can cause them to freeze and panic. The difference between great leaders and ineffective executives is that a great leader helps solve difficult problems.

THE BOTTOM LINE

» See beyond the restrictions holding you and your team back, and *do more with less.*

NEXT STEPS

1. Take a major project you are already working on and backtrack to review its key assumptions. What could change to maximize results?

2. If your next team project seems undoable to some team members, respond with positive energy and schedule a thirty-minute brainstorming session where everyone think of one thing the team can do to move the project forward.

TWENTY–SEVEN

SOLVING COMPLEX PROBLEMS

I got inspiration for the *3 Minute Mentor* content from a variety of places. The most common source of inspiration came from situations I faced as a manager and executive with my team, and questions I got at work. I also saw a great many ineffective and ineffectual employees and managers in my day. These individuals and their struggles provided the genesis for content.

One situation that got me really mad highlighted the difficulty people have in solving complex problems. In this case, a project had gone so badly that it required a "postmortem" on the situation. (Senior executives always want to review things that go badly.) In this case, they delegated the review to one of their high-potential employees.

The expectation was that this individual would know what to do next. Although these fast-track professionals often know how to solve problems where they control all the elements involved, not all problems, including this one, fall into that category.

One of the hardest and most intimidating situations for any manager to face is a complex problem with no readily apparent solution. Simply figuring out where to start can be daunting. The worst thing to do in this situation is to focus too quickly on doing something—anything—to get started. You might hit upon a good solution right away. More likely, you will find yourself doing the wrong things and having to start over. Or, you might make the problem worse.

Walter, our hero in this example, had to find the root cause of, and the right solution for, an execution problem. Walter got the assignment because he was viewed as a strong problem-solver. True to his nature and reputation, Walter dived right into finding a solution to the problem.

However, Walter did not do anything else. He did not lay the foundation for solving the problem, such as the timeline for doing so, who would be involved, or even the expectations for any eventual solution. As a result, Walter ended up floundering around for several weeks before finally asking for help. Suddenly, a high-performance, high-profile, twenty-first employee had become a Stuck-in-the-Middle one!

As it happened, Walter came to me for feedback on what he was doing wrong and advice on what to do instead. The first thing I told him was to stop what he was doing immediately. Walter needed to lay the foundation for his problem-solving effort.

My point was that even if Walter had developed a solution through his initial efforts, chances were good that this solution would not have taken hold because he did not prepare the groundwork for its success. To use a homebuilding analogy, Walter's approach was akin to designing the bathroom before pouring the foundation or laying out the floor plan.

LAY A TEN-STEP FOUNDATION

A better approach to solving a complex problem is to develop a plan for doing so that will support the overall effort. When I face a complex problem, I start the process of solving it with ten steps.

No matter how much or how little time you have to solve a problem, going through these ten steps ultimately saves you time and effort.

1. Stop and plan first. No matter how tempted you are to dive right into problem-solving, don't. You need to accept that some preplanning is in order and make time for it. Finding solutions to complex problems requires structure, teamwork, and planning. If you do not take the time at the beginning to plan, you will waste a lot time along the way. This initial planning is better done with a small team or even just two people. Getting the basic objectives and end-date for the project up front is important because they may be nonnegotiable. This is something you cannot do in a big group.

2. Identify your customer. You are solving this problem for a reason: to provide a product for the end user. Therefore, you will present your solution to the end user. Be clear on who that person is and what you need to deliver to them and when. In addition to the end user, you should also keep in mind the key influencers of that end user who are also likely to be interested in your solution.

3. Detail expectations. Once you know who your end users and other important influencers are, you work with those individuals to articulate their expectations for your work and the outcome of the entire project, including timelines and review cycles. Write down these elements and copy them back to the people who provided that information. Projects often are viewed as failing not because the work was bad, but because they did not meet the requester's expectations. Also, now is the time to ask who else should be involved in, and working on, the project.

4. Lay out the timelines. Next, lay out the whole timeline for the project, including checkpoints, reviews, and final presentations. With this timeline in mind, you book required time on the calendars of those involved in the project. While your project may be the hottest thing going on today, who knows what might happen tomorrow. Get those calendar slots before someone else does. I have seen projects fail simply because the project had no timelines. In some cases, the end user or project manager has a timeline expectation in his head, but does not take the time to articulate and communicate that timeline to others. If you are struggling with this, start at the end and work backwards from the delivery date.

5. Assemble the team. As you assemble the cross-functional team necessary to complete the project and solve the problem, keep in mind that these people have other priorities and responsibilities. Therefore, you need to sell them on the importance of being part of the team, rather than simply telling them that they have to serve. Otherwise, you may never get the necessary buy-in and support from those team members. *Look for the people with the right content, approach, and network, and not just those at the "right" level in the organization.* Gathering a room full of vice presidents does not necessarily mean you have found the right people to get the work done. While managing multilevel teams is often harder, it is a great skill for a 21st Century Executive to have.

6. Agree on the objectives. Once the team is in place, the team as a whole should work together to define and agree on objectives. You may already have objectives in mind, but the team should ratify your plans. Remember, a critical purpose of the team is to gain collective wisdom. That means the team may want to change some of your objectives. This process is a good exercise in team bonding. However, do not allow individual members to distract you from the ultimate goals. Do not forget that while good objectives should stretch the team, they must be quantifiable, real, and achievable.

7. Detail your assumptions. Any problem-solving approach requires the team to make certain assumptions about unknown elements of the problem. To make sure those assumptions are appropriate, the team needs to detail and test those assumptions with the sponsors and decision makers involved in the project. The resulting clarity and agreement will help to improve the final output. For example, a problem involving production issues might require assumptions about quality levels and output volumes.

8. Understand the strategy process. Problem solving requires a strategy to guide the effort. Pursuing the wrong strategy often means that the team will waste a lot of time on irrelevant details because it is not sure exactly where it is going or the best way to get there. For more information of the strategy process, see Chapter 29.

9. Delegate data collection. Problem solving requires data. Teams must quickly assess what data they need and then divide the workload evenly to go about collecting it. If ten people are on the team, all ten of those team members should take on an equal share of required data collection.

10. Be the captain of the team — not the commandant. Bringing the team together is just the beginning of this problem-solving process. Keeping the team working together is an ongoing challenge. You need to be a hands-on leader who works alongside the members of the team. You cannot dip in and out of the sessions acting like you are simply the final reviewer checking their work.

If you have ever seen the movie *Apollo 13* that depicted efforts to bring home astronauts from space following a breakdown in crucial equipment, you have seen this type of prepared problem solving in action (even allowing for the inevitable artistic license taken). In that case, the Mission Control commander:

1. Stopped, however briefly, to plan;
2. Identified the end user (NASA, the astronauts, the general public);
3. Detailed the expectations (bring the astronauts home alive);
4. Clarified timelines (how long they had to bring the astronauts home safely);
5. Assembled the team necessary to achieve the goal;
6. Agreed on objectives throughout the project;
7. Detailed the assumptions based on what was known about the situation and its limitations;
8. Understood the strategy process involved;
9. Delegated data collection to various team members based on their expertise and availability;
10. Acted as the leader of the team to keep it together until the situation was successfully resolved.

Not every situation will be as critical as the one experienced by the *Apollo 13* astronauts. However, your approach to solving problems will tell those around you a lot about your capabilities as a manager and a 21st Century Executive.

THE BOTTOM LINE

» As the old saying goes, "He who fails to plan, plans to fail."

Next Steps

1. Think about a current project and why it may not be moving as fast as it could be. Did the project team miss any of the ten foundation-laying steps?

2. When someone asks you to give input into a project, make sure your advice is in the context of these ten steps.

3. Next time you are involved or are leading a formal project, make sure you follow the ten foundation-laying steps first.

TWENTY-EIGHT

TELLING SOMEONE
TO DO SOMETHING

Part of being a manager is telling people to do things—complete tasks, draft reports, make changes, and so on. Sometimes, people are fine with doing what you ask of them. Sometimes, they are not. In the latter case, the situation could require difficult conversations and test your mettle as a manager.

A 21st Century Executive needs to be prepared to hold these conversations effectively, especially when these conversations promise to be difficult. Only a Stuck-in-the-Middle Manager runs away from a difficult conversation.

Tammy, a manager who reported to me, had to tell one of her team members, Bert, that he was going to work with another team for a period of time. The problem was that Bert did not like the members of the other team (let's call them Team B) and resisted the move. Because Team B faced a critical deadline that it could not miss under any circumstances, Tammy had no choice but to move Bert to Team B.

Unfortunately, Bert dragged his feet and continued to work at his old desk on issues related to Tammy's team. He essentially ignored Tammy's request to move to Team B. If Tammy was a Stuck-in-the-Middle Manager, she would have ignored the situation and let Bert do what he wanted in order to avoid a difficult conversation.

Tammy recognized her responsibility to have Bert do what was needed. Tammy felt she had only two options for handling this situation: 1) she could give Bert an ultimatum in which he could move to Team B or he would have to face disciplinary issues; or, 2) she could have a difficult conversation with Bert about why he needed to make this move and help Team B. Because Tammy believed that Bert was not going to move to Team B without a compelling reason, she did not want to box herself into a situation where she had to discipline a valuable team member. Not only did Tammy want to avoid any legal issues involved, but she also knew taking this tack would not solve Team B's problem.

Tammy ultimately had a frank discussion with Bert about why he did not want to work with Team B and why he was resisting the change. To make sure this conversation was a success, Tammy had to prepare carefully to make sure that the discussion ended with Bert moving to Team B and supporting that team's efforts.

When they held that meeting, Bert aired his reasons for not wanting to work on Team B. For her part, Tammy explained why Bert's efforts were crucial to Team B's project *and to the company as a whole*. Tammy gave Bert clear direction so that he understood what was required of him. In fact, she repeated that requirement three times. Then she asked Bert a series of questions, knowing his answers would indicate if Bert was completely clear and understood that he had no choice but to move to Team B and to give that team his best effort.

MAKING DIFFICULT CONVERSATIONS EASIER

No one enjoys this type of conversation, but there are times when these conversations are necessary. When you find yourself in one of those situations, there are some ways to make having that difficult conversation easier.

EXPLAIN WHY THE ISSUE IS SO IMPORTANT

There are typically two ways difficult conversations get started. The conversation with Bert became necessary because a manager needed an employee to do something and the employee resisted. When you, as a manager or 21st Century Executive, initiate such a conversation, you need to emphasize the importance of your request and continually restate it until it is completely clear to the employee.

You need to make sure that your message is heard and understood. At the same time, you need to remain open to listening to the employee's concerns about the request and the situation overall. *Whatever you do, do not go in unprepared.* Think through, and be able to articulate, why your request is important. Have two or three clear reasons ready to discuss. Although it can be tempting to simply say, "Because I said so," you are not talking to an employee who is twelve years old and refusing to clean his bedroom.

If the employee initiates this type of conversation, you must be prepared to deal with the issues the employee raises. In this situation, you do not have as much time to prepare, but you can buy some time as you ask questions. Before you speak, be clear that you really understand what your employee is asking. While the employee has put you on the "hot spot," you do not have to stay there. If necessary, take a time-out or break to think through what the employee is asking for and, if necessary, seek help or advice.

At some point, no matter how the conversation started, it must end. If the two parties cannot agree on an outcome, the employee may just have to "suck it up" and do what is required. If the employee continues to resist the request, you make completely clear to the employee the consequences of that refusal, whatever they may be. *It is important not to end the meeting until both parties agree upon a specific action and the date by when the action must occur.*

Focus on Having a Productive Conversation

If you are initiating this type of difficult conversation, these six steps can help ensure that the conversation is effective.

1. Small talk: start with small talk to get the conversation going and to help the employee relax. Do not take too long to get to the meat of the conversation; conversely, jumping in too fast often makes both of you defensive. A couple of minutes of idle chatter should be enough.

2. Questioning and exploring: ask an appropriate series of questions that explore the area you will be discussing. If the employee is failing at a role, these questions should not be too obscure or difficult. Ask about the outputs the employee thinks are needed. If the employee is doing something wrong, ask about any relationships or issues with the people involved. Listen carefully to the employee's answers.

In the situation between Bert and Tammy, Bert's reluctance to join Team B was the result of a bad experience Bert had several months earlier with Team B's leader. By asking pointed questions about this experience, Tammy got a clear picture of Bert's concerns.

3. Identifying the gap: if you are asking the right questions, you will start to see the gap between what you want and what the employee understands or is doing. Using the insight she gained from their conversations, Tammy realized that Bert was concerned that Team B's leader would not give Bert full credit for anything he did for Team B, or worse (in Bert's mind), Bert would be "stuck" working for Team B after the project was over.

4. Clarifying the needs: when you have a clear idea of where the gap is and the extent of it, clearly express to the employee what needs to be done and what the employee needs to do differently. If necessary, repeat the request or action until you think the employee gets it. If you are not sure, ask the employee to repeat back what you have asked. Tammy focused this part of the conversation on reassuring Bert that the change to Team B would be short-term, and that Tammy would be monitoring the situation and Bert's treatment by Team B's leader to make sure everything was going well.

5. Checking for comprehension: once you have clearly stated what you need the employee to do, give the employee an opportunity to ask questions to get clarity about your request. If these questions indicate that the employee still does not understand what you want and what the employee must do, continue the conversation until the employee is clear on those things.

6. Agree on follow-up: once everything is understood, agree on a date to check on the employee's progress. For Bert, this was perhaps the most important part of the conversation. To reinforce her commitment to getting Bert back to his team as soon as possible, Tammy put in writing that Bert's assignment to Team B was short-term in nature and that he would be transferred back as soon as Team B's project was over. This reassured Bert that the move would not be permanent, and that Tammy would be looking out for him.

The same steps apply when the employee initiates the conversation. The only difference is that you do not necessarily have the same amount of time to prepare. When that happens, remember to ask questions and listen to the answers. Do not jump in to solve the employee's problem until you really understand it.

BE CLEAR

These conversations do not always generate the desired results. The employee may leave the conversation with one idea of what the manager wants and expects, and the manager may leave thinking she has communicated something else entirely.

Problems with miscommunication occur when managers are not completely clear on the desired outcome. If you try to soften the message or your delivery by talking around the problem, you will simply "muddy" the message. This approach will not do you or the other person any favors.

To have a successful conversation, you must be unambiguous about the outcome you want, and say it simply. It is better to be a little too blunt than to have any misunderstanding. Tammy made it very clear to Bert that refusing to move to Team B would be extremely detrimental to his career, particularly since Bert was in line to assume a team leader role when one opened up. If Tammy had been less clear, Bert might have come away from the conversation with the idea that he could somehow still avoid moving to Team B or make the move but give less than 100 percent.

Remember, if the employee does not get what you are trying to say, the fault ultimately lies with *you*—and not with the employee.

THE BOTTOM LINE

» In a difficult conversation, be clear and direct about the outcome you want, and do not end the conversation until you and the employee agree on a specific action and date.

NEXT STEPS

1. Commit to having difficult conversations when necessary. Watch yourself to make sure that you are not avoiding them.

2. Before a difficult conversation, brainstorm some potential solutions to alleviate an employee's reluctance to what you are going to propose.

3. Once you have had the difficult conversation, check in with the employee a week and then a month later to see if you are both still on the same page.

TWENTY-NINE

BUILDING A STRATEGY

We began this book with a quote from *Alice in Wonderland* that can be paraphrased as follows: *If you don't know where you are going, it doesn't matter which road you take.* A 21st Century Executive always has an idea of where he is trying to go.

The same principle applies when it comes to building a strategy. Great strategies often fail because they are not built on a strong foundation.

Several years ago, I joined a team as it planned its strategy for the coming year. The meeting began with an energetic discussion of the team's current problems with the budgeting process, the size of the budget, and its struggles with the finance and accounting team. The team could not get past the problems it was having that day even though the purpose of the meeting was to develop a strategy for the future.

To get the team back on the meeting's purpose, I suggested that the team stop worrying about this year and focus on where they wanted to be in three years. I began asking some key questions about overall objectives, investments for specific big line items, programs to fund, and the resources we needed to pursue the articulated strategy.

By focusing on the future first, the team stopped obsessing over the current situation. The team discovered that it would not require some of the processes and procedures they had been using. Therefore, any energy spent worrying about those issues would be wasted.

To build an effective strategy with a strong foundation, you need to follow some simple rules:

1. Decide where you want to go and what you want to accomplish.
2. Describe where you are.
3. Determine how to get from where you are to where you want to be.

You can use this approach to develop a strategy for a business, a career, or your personal life. Once you, your team, or your company has a destination in mind, you can focus on getting there instead of obsessing over the problems and issues you currently face.

STEP 1:

DECIDE WHERE YOU WANT TO GO

AND WHAT YOU WANT TO DO

To build an effective strategy, first be clear about your final destination. This is the time to describe the future using concrete terms and metrics. A career strategy might focus on achieving a certain job or level in an organization with specific responsibilities and power. A business strategy might focus on market position, using specific metrics, definitions, and milestones. Use whatever makes sense to your team or your role, but make it numeric.

The time period for arriving at this destination should be far enough in the future in order to give you enough time to execute the strategy. In most cases, this is three to five years. When building a business plan, you should ask yourself what market share you would like to achieve within three years or what it would take to be the market leader.

If you are building a strategy for your career, you may want to focus on the level you would like to attain, how much money you want to earn, what you want to accomplish or invent, or whatever you think your key motivation is. *In both business and personal situations, be careful to find the balance between the easy and the impossible.*

When you deciding on a strategy for your team, choose targets that are real and achievable—but clearly designed to stretch the team.

This is not to say that the strategy or the metrics cannot change over time. Nonetheless, the planning process should always start with a specific timeframe and goal.

STEP 2:
DESCRIBE WHERE YOU ARE

Part of the strategy-building process is to remove yourself from the day-to-day issues that will cause you to miss your objectives. This is more challenging for some people than others. Many teams and individuals waste an enormous amount of time focusing on where they are currently. Once you know where you want to go, articulating where you are currently relative to that destination is much easier. *Frame the conversation by the goal instead of the details of your current daily life.*

Using the metrics defined in Step 1, the team can determine where it stands today on each metric. Current problems now become issues to be solved or overcome as the team moves forward, rather than a current conflict where everyone wants to assign blame.

You should dedicate the shortest amount of time to this part of building your strategy. At this point, where you are starting from is all that matters. Keep the focus off why moving forward will be so difficult.

STEP 3:

WORK OUT HOW TO GET FROM
TODAY TO TOMORROW

In the end, *building a strategy is about how you get from today to tomorrow, including the plans and actions needed to achieve the success you seek.* By focusing on how to get from where the team is today to where it wants to be in the future, the focus moves away from the problems of today. This is where the team forms its strategy.

Laying out milestones to be reached along the way breaks down the journey into manageable pieces. Putting names and dates to each milestone creates accountability and urgency. Metrics can help guide the team's actions.

You may find yourself with a team that is stuck in the "tyranny of today." In other words, while the team can set an objective and define its present state, the team cannot see past day-to-day problems to work on the steps of the strategy.

When my team is stuck or I am stuck in this position, I run a Critical Success Factors (CSF) exercise. I ask the team to write down three things that must happen for us to be successful. The focus is not on the actions but on the outcome. Typically, this process delivers answers like "launch our product on time," "train the sales force," or "build a channel capability."

As a group, we review all of these actions and prioritize the top ten or so. While this exercise can take a couple of hours, we typically end with a list of things that need to be done. We can then go through each one, listing the actions needed, the personnel responsible, and the date for completion. Without knowing it, we will have built the strategy and will be well along the way to defining the execution plan. With all of those elements in place in one plan, a team now has a tool by which to execute, measure, and manage itself.

You can also run a CSF exercise as a stand-alone activity. I recently worked with a team that had been asked to detail a marketing strategy around the 4Ps — Product, Pricing, Promotion, and Placement (or distribution strategy). While the team members understood what this meant, they had never approached their work that way.

Rather than diving down into each of the 4Ps with the team, we ran a CSF exercise. The team quickly identified twelve things necessary to help them achieve their objectives. With that list, the team saw that the twelve could be sorted into a number of categories, including the 4Ps. From there, the team started working on the actions or strategies needed to build the plan.

THE BOTTOM LINE

» The road, or strategy, you should take gets you from where you are today to where you want to be tomorrow.

NEXT STEPS

1. Think about your current career strategy. Can you list the objectives that reflect where you want to be in three years?

2. Look at this year's objectives for your team, and run a team CSF exercise.

3. Next time you need to build a strategy, commit to following the three steps — but keep the discussion of Step 2 brief!

THIRTY

THE ART OF DELEGATING

As we have seen in our At Work survey, a gap often exists between how people judge themselves and how they judge others. Delegation is no different. Our survey showed that 69 percent of the respondents think they are "good" or "extremely good at delegating," but 55 percent think their peers and their bosses are "average" or "worse" at delegating.

We all know that no manager can be successful without learning to delegate. Those who resist delegation almost always turn out to be practitioners of Stuck-in-the-Middle Management.

Being an effective leader requires choosing the right people to do what you do not have time or skills to do yourself in order to complete a project, mandate, or mission. Effective delegation is the foundation of strong management.

Indeed, one of the benefits of being a manager in the twenty-first century is you don't have to have the skills your people have. At one point, I had four hundred people reporting to me! I did not know how to do things like web analysis, so I had people on my team who could do that for me. *At some point, you simply have to delegate to be effective.*

As you move into more senior management positions, you start to understand that delegating is more than getting people to do work for you. Delegating is also a tool to encourage your people to stretch their creative muscles and develop new skills. Even if you have the time and skill to do something, still delegate to someone who will see tasks and projects as a development opportunity.

Delegating the Right Way

All 21st Century Executives need to delegate correctly.

A few years ago, I worked with Bob, a manager who was new to his position and to management. Bob's team was working on part of an important product development project. One of Bob's first actions as manager was to delegate a portion of the project to two team members, Jim and Sarah.

When the critical action date came, Jim and Sarah presented their work to Bob. Unfortunately, although both Jim and Sarah had worked hard, their work wasn't in the required format. Bob could not share it with the full product development team until the work was redone correctly. Time was lost, Bob ended up missing a key deadline, and he vented his frustration on Jim and Sarah.

Bob created this problem himself. When Bob delegated this work, he neglected to tell Jim and Sarah that the product development team was using a very specific format to collect information and data. As a result, Jim and Sarah used the team's usual format for their work instead of the specific format required by the product development team.

Bob's attempt to delegate failed because he had not thought through what he needed from Jim and Sarah, nor had he communicated his needs effectively. Bob might have saved himself if he had added a mid-project review to his plan so that he could have caught the error early on.

Delegation is a bit like a train. If you put a train on the right track, it will go in the direction you want it to go. If you don't put the train on the right track, you do not know where it will end up. Bob did not put Jim and Sarah on the right track.

Effective delegation is a three-part process. By answering the following simple questions, Bob could have delegated with a much better outcome.

1. When should you delegate, and to whom?

There are generally three reasons to delegate something—to save time, to leverage someone else's skills, and to provide staff with development opportunities. The reason you are delegating will determine to whom you delegate.

Saving time: there are only so many hours in a day. If the workload is getting too large, effective managers look for ways to shift some tasks and responsibilities to others on their teams. Bob chose to delegate to Jim and Sarah because both had just completed a project and had more free time than other team members.

Accessing skills: as a manager, you hold responsibility for delivering work even when you personally do not have the skills to complete that work. A manager who does not have the skills to complete certain projects or tasks must find someone on her team or in other areas of the organization who does.

Developing staff: a critical reason for delegating is to give others a chance to develop and try out new skills. Even if those people don't do things as quickly as you or someone more experienced might, these opportunities are strategic to these team members' growth. Choosing these individuals should be based on who needs or wants the opportunity and whether they are ready for it.

2. WHAT IS THE BEST WAY TO DELEGATE?

Delegating does not mean simply handing or e-mailing someone a file and telling her when you need the work done. Even if you do not care how they get the job done, do not assume your team members know what you want. This is the mistake Bob made.

Bob (and Jim and Sarah) would have had a much better outcome with defined requirements.

Effective managers set a framework for the delegated task that includes the following information:

1. The deadline for completion.
2. Any required input that must be included in the finished product.
3. The people they need to consult and the processes they must follow.
4. How the output should be delivered and to whom.
5. The authority the person has to do the job.

If you don't want to take the time to provide this information, you need to be prepared to accept what you get.

3. WHAT ARE THE POTENTIAL PROBLEMS?

The basis of any management job is delegation. As a manager, you need to manage your own expectations when it comes to delegating. Even when you delegate the authority to complete a task or project to a team member, the responsibility still ultimately resides with you. Managers who worry about the quality of work they are going to get back need to move beyond those concerns. As a manager, you cannot do the work of the whole team.

I remember having a team member who gave me back the work I had delegated to him at the last minute. During the ensuing discussion, I asked if he completed his assignments as he got them or always waited until the deadline. He told me he often had to "pull an all-nighter" because that is how he worked best. Because I work the opposite way and work on projects as I get them, we had to learn how to work together effectively. What is more, I had to learn how to adjust my approach and expectations when I delegated to him in order to manage my own stress levels. Each person you delegate to will receive the work and respond to you in a different way. You have to adjust to that.

Important to remember about delegation is that *you cannot delegate responsibility in your boss's eyes. You still will own any failure that occurs no matter who did the actual work.* Few executives will want to hear you blame people on your or anyone else's team. At the same time, the team member who successfully completes a delegated task or project must still get credit for that success.

Finally, pay attention to *cascading delegation,* where a task or project you delegate in turn gets delegated to others. The senior vice president gives it to the vice president, who gives it to the director, who in turn delegates it to a manager, who passes it on to his team. The poor gal or guy at the end is so far removed from the original request it becomes almost impossible for him or her to fulfill the task. In addition, if the work is then "handled" by someone at every level, the final deliverable will probably not look anything like the work that was done originally. When this has happened to me, I usually discovered that the task or project was delegated without my knowledge to someone who did not have the skills to complete the work.

In those situations, I did not get what I needed, and we had to start all over again.

THE BOTTOM LINE

» Effective delegation is the foundation of strong management, and a basic skill of any 21st Century Executive.

NEXT STEPS

1. If you typically are a hands-on-every-detail manager, challenge yourself to be hands-off by delegating five tasks you normally handle. Then limit yourself to weekly check-ins on the projects with your employees.

2. Delete an appropriate task to the new employee on the team. Assess the strength of the newcomer's skill set when the task is complete.

3. At an upcoming team meeting, discuss the concept of *cascading delegation*, and identify when it is important for your team members to highlight to you when they have passed on an assigned task.

THIRTY-ONE

MANAGING HORIZONTALLY

One of the most important skills you need as a manager is *the ability to manage people who do not work for you.* If you handle this type of *horizontal management* well, more senior people in the company will take note. As a result, you will not only be able to do your job better, you will increase your overall influence within the organization and enhance your career prospects.

On the flip side, if you fail to manage horizontally, this shortcoming can derail even the most promising career. I have seen many otherwise promising managers get passed over for new roles because those individuals are perceived as unable to work well with, or to influence, their peers. *If someone says to you that you "do not play well with others," pay attention.* What that person is really saying is that you are not able to be effective when it comes to managing horizontally.

In one of my roles as a senior executive, I worked with a team leader who was in charge of a product development team. The team was formed to bring a new product to market. In this case, Carol, the team leader, needed not only to manage her team, but she also needed contributions from other resources throughout the company in order to deliver the new product. Specifically, she needed help from finance, marketing, legal, engineering, and production.

Carol recognized that these resources were external to her team; moreover, these resources neither worked for the team nor had much of a stake in her team's success. Additionally, these individuals had many other priorities above and beyond what Carol needed them to do in order for her team to achieve its goals and mandate.

To deal with this situation, Carol worked hard to convince those individuals that working with her product development team would be advantageous to the company and to their own careers. Carol emphasized the importance of the product the team was developing, its potential sales, the size of its market, and the potential for additional add-on products that would ensure the company a strong position in one of its key markets.

Thanks to Carol's ability to recognize the need to manage horizontally and her effective approach in doing so, the team achieved its goals and delivered the product on time. After the project was over, management, who had always seen Carol as a particularly effective manager and leader, took a fresh look at Carol's accomplishments and positioned her for quick promotion.

THE KEYS TO EFFECTIVE HORIZONTAL MANAGEMENT

Carol's approach is a classic example of horizontal management. If you want to become an effective horizontal manager, you need to understand the following:

1. WHY IT IS NECESSARY TO MANAGE HORIZONTALLY?

Cross-functional teams are an excellent way to accomplish any number of objectives. In certain situations, a cross-functional team is the only way to achieve an objective. Yet these teams also create challenges for managers and team leaders.

First of all, few cross-functional teams are complete with only their core members. Nearly every team must rely on the sporadic or part-time contributions of specialists from various areas of the company.

When this happens, the manager of that team, like Carol, must find ways to work with and manage people who do not work for her. The worst thing a manager can do is to use this fact as an excuse to give up management responsibility. At the same time, no team leader can expect to have management responsibility for everyone who contributes to the team. Such an approach would bog down the team and the team leader, and frankly, would not be a viable solution.

I have known people working in senior level jobs who are under the mistaken impression that a team cannot leverage someone as a project resource unless that person works directly for the team leader or manager. Any manager or executive who operates under this assumption is basically focusing on organizational issues at the expense of the team's objectives or plan, and is a classic example of a Stuck-in-the-Middle Manager.

If an organization allows such assumptions to lead to a reorganization, it is likely to find that the reorganization solved nothing and did not improve the performance of the affected teams. The reason? The reorganization did not address the root problem. The managers and leaders who called for the reorganization are still unable to influence people or to manage people who don't report to them.

2. THE BASIC PRINCIPLES OF HORIZONTAL MANAGEMENT

Horizontal management requires leadership that springs from having authority rather than power. You must find ways to motivate people to work with you and to become an active and contributing part of the team. You cannot expect to succeed by just telling these people what to do. You do not have the power to make someone do something just because you asked.

In a few cases, a manager may well honor your request simply based on your personal relationship with that manager. However, you cannot count on that happening. Even if a manager does it once, you cannot expect people to keep providing resources indefinitely without any benefit to themselves.

Let's look more closely at how Carol used horizontal management to ensure her team had access to the necessary resources from other teams. *These steps apply in just about any horizontal management situation where you are trying to influence another team or individual to do something, or not do something.*

- **Make the case.** Carol relied on what I like to call the "Three Ms" — mission, metrics, and milestones — for the broader effort and not just her own team. Carol was very clear not only about what she had to achieve, but the impact and value of her team's work to the whole organization. The ability to articulate the broader value of what you are doing and trying to achieve is critical.
- **Understand others' objectives.** Understanding how teams' objectives overlap, and how a resource request can lead to joint success, is crucial to successful horizontal management. For that reason, Carol made sure she understood the objectives of the teams she needed to work with and from which she needed to draw resources. Other managers are not likely to give up resources to work on projects that

are either peripheral to, or that work against, their basic objectives. By understanding the other team's objectives, Carol was well positioned to tailor her requests and articulate her priorities so that they meshed with the other manager's objectives.

- **Ask for what you need, and no more.** The next challenge is to be clear and honest about the resources you need—how much, of what type, and for how long. Once Carol provided this information, the other manager was able to assess the impact of the request on his own deliverables. Few managers are likely to agree to an open-ended resource request. It is important to explain why the team should not hire its own resources, and an opened-ended request only serves to undermine your argument.
- **Justify the request.** You need to justify your resource request. Carol made the case for her resource request using the broader objectives of her team's work, the other team's overlapping objectives, and her actual resource request. Armed with similar information, you can work directly with the other manager to fulfill your requests. The best approach is to meet with the manager face-to-face if possible. E-mail is too easy for the other manager to avoid and ignore, especially if he does not want to give you what you want.

At this point, if your case for your request is limited to the fact that you do not have a particular resource on the team or that you do not have the budget to hire that resource, you need to rethink your request until you can come up with a more compelling argument.

3. HOW TO ENSURE SUCCESS

Once your resource requests have been fulfilled and you have all of the necessary resources on board, the next step in horizontal management is to make sure that the teams involved and senior management understand, endorse, and support the specifics of the team's mission, metrics, and milestones.

By creating a regular review process to gauge progress on the mission, metrics, and milestones, the team leader can communicate that progress to the entire team, any other individuals working with the team, and senior management. Finally, the team leader needs to make sure that team members have defined responsibilities that are clearly linked to the team's mission, metrics, and milestones.

As the team leader focuses on achieving the defined milestones, it is important to make sure everyone on the team and the individuals who are working with and supporting the team continue to work toward those milestones. If someone is not executing as needed, the team leader will need to escalate the situation to a higher level of management to make sure everything is being executed as needed and on schedule. See Chapter 27 for how to escalate.

THE BOTTOM LINE

» Play well with others and you move ahead; play by yourself and you will watch your promising career derail.

NEXT STEPS

1. Think through the last resource request you approved or denied, and consider the key factors in that decision.

2. Map out which of your peers has objectives and deliverables that overlap with yours, then seek out their help and assistance as appropriate.

3. Next time someone asks you for resources, ask how delivering on that request will allow you to meet some of your or your team's objectives.

THIRTY-TWO

ORGANIZATIONAL SAVVY

Managers require many "soft" skills to succeed in their work and careers. One of those soft skills is *organizational savvy*. Without organizational savvy, it is very easy to fall into a pattern of Stuck-in-the-Middle Management.

Ralph, one of my direct reports, was very good at his work. One day, Ralph confided in me that his ultimate ambition was to become an executive. As nicely as I could, I told Ralph that I did not think he would ever achieve that goal because he lacked organizational savvy.

Here is why Ralph fell short in organizational savvy: first, Ralph always spoke his mind during meetings regardless of who was in the room. Anyone who wants to be an executive must develop emotional intelligence to know what to say, when to say it, and to whom. If Ralph had an obvious question to which he should have known the answer or a question with the potential to embarrass a colleague, he would just ask it in front of the group rather than waiting to ask someone one-to-one later on. When he spoke up in front of senior staff, his words often reflected badly on him.

Second, although Ralph always finished his projects, the process he went through to do so was very messy from an organizational standpoint. Frustrated by this, people would leave his project teams before completion. Ralph would then abruptly ask his managers to assign additional resources to his projects. Also, he worked his project teams very hard to meet deadlines that were too ambitious.

When I asked Ralph about this behavior, he told me that he thought it was good to "break glass" to get things done. I told him that while I understood his intentions, if he were ever to become more than an individual contributor and make it to the executive suite, he could not have "dead bodies scattered around" at the end of his projects.

If Ralph had a greater level of organizational savvy, he would have found ways to complete his projects more efficiently and cleanly, and he would have understood when to speak his mind and when to keep his own counsel.

What Is Organizational Savvy?

Organizational savvy is the political antennae that you need to operate successfully in any organization. It is part reading and understanding people's emotions and behaviors, and part understanding how an entire team, department, or organization operates.

Like people, organizations can be happy or sad, motivated or destructive. Employees who are organizationally savvy can read individual and organizational emotions, and tailor their behavior accordingly. People and organizations expect a certain type of behavior in many cases. If you do not understand those expectations and act in keeping with those expectations, you can hamper your ability to be effective in an organization and to influence people.

If Ralph had cultivated his organizational savvy, he would have understood or asked for guidance on how to manage his projects and his meeting behavior to fit with the expectations of his organization. If he operated under that insight, people would have paid more attention to what Ralph said, would have seen the value in his projects, would have worked more readily, and would have been more open to Ralph's influence.

Being able to read and channel individual and organizational emotion means that you have organizational savvy.

WHY IS ORGANIZATIONAL SAVVY IMPORTANT?

Influencing people is a crucial part of being a manager. Also, the ability to influence an entire organization is important. If you lack organizational savvy, you will lack the ability to command the attention and respect necessary to influence an organization's actions and decision-making.

Just as you adapt your style based on your knowledge of the person you are trying to influence, you must also do that at an organizational level. A manager who lacks organizational savvy often assumes that an organization works the way she wants the organization to work. To influence an entire organization, you must be able to tune into the organization's psyche—not just its culture—to understand that organization and how it works.

Ralph was particularly weak in this area. His perception of how things should work in the organization was so far from the reality of how that organization operated on a daily basis that he was constantly annoying people with his requests and ways of working. He was generally swimming "against the tide."

Some people might consider organizational savvy as being political. Political instincts are part of what organizational savvy requires. That is not necessarily a bad thing.

How Do You Become Savvy?

Developing organizational savvy requires listening and observing. With time, you will see patterns in the organization's behavior. At this point, you need to consider how your own style and leadership approach mesh with the organization's rhythms. If things happen in a low-key fashion, you cannot expect to be successful with a brash leadership style.

Before you move forward on anything in an organization—particularly one that is new to you—you should do so in a way that is consistent with your impression of the organization's way of operating. Once you do that, see what happens and how people respond, then adapt your approach based on what you learn and try again.

The more you do this and use these experiences to understand other people and their motivations, the more organizational savvy you will develop. *This is not a one-time process, but a lifelong and career-long pattern of learning and adapting.*

Can You Gain Personal Organizational Savvy?

If you are not in a position to influence an entire organization, you should be developing political antennae that allow you to sense what is happening on a smaller scale. For example, in a meeting or at a conference, you should start testing your organizational savvy and analyzing the results.

By processing and being aware of your environment in this way, you learn when to ask questions and when not to, when to speak and when to be silent, and when to push and when to push back.

Building this type of organizational savvy is akin to post-graduate work for managers and executives. Organizational savvy emerges from the sum total of all of the skills and nuances you have picked up throughout your career.

Your challenge is to forge all of those things together over time. Organizations, like people, change and grow, so you need to keep your organizational savvy current. You must constantly keep your finger on the pulse of the organization you are working with or for.

If my colleague Ralph had been able to learn these lessons and develop some level of organizational savvy, his career would have turned out much differently. For all of us, not having or not demonstrating savvy is a classic way of derailing our careers.

THE BOTTOM LINE

» As the song says, "You got to know when to hold 'em. Know when to fold 'em. Know when to walk away. Know when to run."

NEXT STEPS

1. Determine who among your peers has the best organizational savvy. Identify something they do that demonstrates it, and see if you can learn from your observation.

2. When you are next in a meeting with executives more senior than you, watch how they read each other and discuss things they disagree with.

THIRTY-THREE

GETTING YOUR TEAM
TO WORK WITH YOU

New managers often face resistance from their team members. This is particularly true when these team members are older and have a longer tenure with the organization. If you do not deal with this type of resistance carefully, you could find yourself struggling to manage the team.

With less experience, new managers tend not to have the tools and insight necessary to deal with this situation. Even experienced 21st Century Executives can struggle at times to find a solution.

When a friend's daughter, Natalie, was assigned to manage a team with several older members, she faced considerable disruption and resistance. Those older team members did not do what Natalie asked them to do. Worse, those individuals undermined Natalie's authority among the other team members.

When Natalie asked me to help her work through the problem, I gave her three pieces of advice:

1. Talk to the disruptive team members.
2. Focus on the work, not on you or the individuals involved.
3. Help team members by removing any obstacles on the job.

Let's look at these three steps and how they helped Natalie deal with her team's resistance.

STEP 1:
TALK TO THE TEAM

By the time I talked to Natalie, she had been avoiding the problems with her team members for some time. If she was not careful, Natalie's career would have stalled out, and she would have become a Stuck-in-the-Middle manager. She would have become ineffectual and powerless—never good signs.

Natalie was trying to drive her team members to work at a different pace, and they were resisting these efforts. Because she was new as a manager, she didn't know how to approach this problem and was afraid of upsetting people or looking weak.

It sounds simple and obvious, but *talking to people is the best way to work out problems*. I advised Natalie to start out by having a one-to-one conversation with each team member.

Any manager is likely to be nervous before such a meeting. Keep in mind that your team members are probably more nervous than you are. In fact, they are probably *more* nervous and concerned about the entire situation—and that may be why they are "acting out."

In addition to hearing what team members had to say during these meetings, Natalie discussed her own feelings and perceptions about the situation with each team member in a nonemotional but personal way.

Whatever the reasons for the team members' actions, you need to use these meetings to find ways to deal with the situation. Here are some tips to get the most from these meetings:

- Begin the meeting by asking the team member how they feel about the work they are doing and how they perceive the new team is working.
- Don't be afraid to press employees to get answers. You have no choice if you want to get to the bottom of things and fix the situation.
- If you still don't get a clear answer, you need to state your own case, including your concerns about the behavior and the overall situation, and its potential impact on team performance.
- Be clear and transparent about how things look from your perspective.
- Keep in mind that you could be part of the problem or that something you are doing is exacerbating the situation.
- Don't be defensive or offended by what team members tell you *no matter what.*
- Your job during these meetings is to listen to each team member and understand all concerns.

Natalie took this advice to heart. She held individual meetings with each team member. In each session, Natalie emphasized that the team needed to find a way to work together effectively. She pressed each team member for insight into the root causes of the current team resistance to her leadership. Each was happy that she had addressed the situation.

STEP 2:
FOCUS ON THE WORK

In all of your interactions with team members, individually or collectively, stay focused on the work, the plan for the team, and the team's performance. Do not make things personal with team members. Above all, don't take things personally yourself.

This was a key issue in Natalie's situation. Team members had made the problem about Natalie's work and management style rather than what the team needed to accomplish. The team members resented having to suddenly work faster than they wanted to work.

Natalie also expected team members to think and act more broadly than before. Rather than simply focusing on team deadlines and efforts, she asked team members to coordinate their deadlines and output with other teams involved in the same area.

Every team has a set of business objectives or a performance plan that should be the sole focus of the team's efforts and conversations. Emphasize that the situation is not about "you and me," but about "the plan." At the same time, it is important not to turn things around and make the plan part of the problem. The plan should be the focus of what you and the team are all doing.

By focusing the conversation on the team's commitment and responsibility to do what the company needed, Natalie shifted the focus onto the work and away from the personalities involved.

STEP 3:
REMOVE OBSTACLES TO TEAM PERFORMANCE

Frequently, teams encounter obstacles to their ability to do their work as expected. It is the manager's job to identify those obstacles and take steps to remove them. When you do this, you show your people that you are on their side and willing to fight for them.

Natalie made identifying and removing obstacles a focus of her conversations with team members. She wanted them to know that she was willing to help them. As a result of the feedback she received during these meetings, Natalie changed the workflow and negotiated with other teams to get deadline extensions as needed.

When people ask me how I approach managing my team and setting objectives for them, I often answer that I do three things: (1) make them work faster than they want to, (2) make them think more broadly that they want to, and (3) help move obstacles out of the way.

If you hire good people who know what they are doing, then the last of these actions is the most valuable. I know managers and leaders who believe in testing their team to see if the team can remove all their own obstacles. There is some value in this approach. For a seasoned leader, it can be a useful experience or test for a team and its members. It is less clear whether this is the best approach for a young or new leader. In many cases, a young leader is better off helping her team by clearing obstacles out the way. If your team members see you as someone who removes obstacles to their own effectiveness and success, they will follow you.

THE BOTTOM LINE

» Be the solution rather than the problem: eliminate team resistance by talking it out and not taking it personally.

NEXT STEPS

1. Schedule a heart-to-heart meeting with any team member who is resisting you or your plan.

2. Think through the obstacles your team is facing, and do what you can do to help the team overcome those obstacles.

THIRTY-FOUR

ENCOURAGING
PRODUCTIVE CONFLICT

Sometimes, you just have to have the fight. Argue it out. Trust me. I've been there.

Conflict is inevitable, but it is not inevitably negative. Although this sounds counterintuitive, tension and friction in the workplace, when addressed effectively, can be important opportunities to foster growth, creativity, and productivity.

It is good to have people challenging each other and challenging themselves. Friction, of course, should not be allowed to turn into warfare. Warfare leads to casualties, and the best way not to become a casualty of war is to avoid going to battle.

If you assume friction and warfare are the same, you will likely encounter unnecessary strife. I suggest approaching conflict as a great opportunity to change or fix something that may have been lingering for a while. *Conflict addressed and conquered could improve and nurture team cohesion.* Hiding it will not make it better.

When I was chief marketing officer of a technology company, I routinely saw conflict between the sales team and the marketing team. Sales focused on short-term, quarterly results, while marketing emphasized long-term product positioning.

In one situation, the sales team wanted to cut pricing to reach year-end sales goals. Marketing fought this out of concern that temporary price reductions would hurt the long-term standing of the affected brands.

In conflicts such as these, there is not necessarily a right or wrong answer. There are, however, several choices. The key is for both sides to work together to identify and evaluate those choices.

To resolve this sales/marketing conflict, the senior leadership team needed to agree on the major priorities for the business over the long term, while determining what parameters the company could put on price and volume in the short, medium, and long terms. By going through that exercise, we were able to align the objectives of the leadership team around those parameters, and the leaders drove their teams accordingly.

To resolve situations like this one positively, both parties need to be transparent and honest about the true nature of the conflict, and then be willing to talk things over and compromise. If the conflict between the sales and marketing teams is actually about something larger than short-term price reductions, such as the overall pricing structure, both sides need to acknowledge that and work on that root problem. Then, they need to share objectives and rewards for making those objectives.

THE NEED FOR TRANSPARENCY

Transparency is the key catalyst for conflict resolution. Resolving conflict requires facts. Until all of the parties involved lay their cards on the table, all of the facts are unlikely to be out in the open.

A great deal of conflict can be traced to a lack of transparency or a lack of openness and honesty somewhere. In the sales/marketing example, the pricing problem began festering when the marketing team made changes to product pricing without involving the sales team or providing the sales team with the rationale for those changes.

This omission was not meant to be malicious or underhanded. The marketing team was simply working through a pricing issue and did not think to include anyone else or to seek feedback from the sales team. For the sales team, the marketing team's action created the appearance that the marketing team was "hiding something."

This situation shows how just a few thoughtless words or actions can look like a conspiracy to others. Unless everyone "comes clean" on what is bothering them, the issues will not be worked out.

What happens when you find yourself in a conflict and you do not think the other party is being transparent? It takes a huge amount of power to make someone be transparent. Unless you have that power, you need to exploit all your influencing skills. In Chapter 23, we talked about some of those skills and how you can change your approach to influence others. Unless the other side is being evil or has a Machiavellian agenda, changing your influencing style can be very effective. Find common ground and work towards a positive outcome for both of you.

The challenge intensifies when people are too idealistic or try to stand on principle. Both approaches suggest some level of immaturity or problems with self-confidence. Or, maybe the individuals are just stubborn or dogmatic. In these situations, you have to consider the role of the management team and how the team members can help you break through. There may just be some things you cannot fix on your own.

TALK IT OUT, COMPROMISE, AND MOVE ON

Every conflict ends in victory, defeat, or a compromise. A victory, in many cases, can be short-lived if the underlying issues are not dealt with. In the parlance of war, *you may win the battle while the war rages on.*

Unless a conflict involves illegal or unethical conduct, *compromise* is almost always the best solution. Responsible business people talk things out. They develop an acceptable compromise so that everyone can move on.

Although this is often difficult because egos and feelings are involved, you have the ability to avoid taking things personally or making things personal. It is your job to keep your focus and your team's focus on the company's objectives.

In the case involving the sales and marketing teams, the leaders of each team agreed early on to talk things through and to keep the discussion focused on the company and its needs. As a result, the teams developed a compromise much faster than they otherwise would.

Be careful not to confuse *compromise* with *consensus*. In business, *consensus* can involve everyone giving consent to an agreement without necessarily agreeing with it. *Compromise* implies a win-win situation where people are both in agreement and willing to execute.

As Dr. Martin Luther King Jr. said, "A genuine leader is not a searcher for consensus but a molder of consensus."

The Bottom Line

» Conflict is everywhere and can be healthy, fostering growth, creativity, and productivity.

Next Steps

1. Next time you are in a situation of conflict, do not dwell on potential bad outcomes. Use any friction as an opportunity to foster transparency, compromise, and growth.

2. If your team supports a different position from that of another team, figure out where you have common goals or objectives, and use them to figure out a compromise. Thereafter, work in tandem.

3. If an issue is resolved and a plan of action determined, consider whether there are any individuals who remain unhappy. *Have they given their consent, but do not agree with the decision?* Then call those team members or colleagues, and promise to provide them with status reports along the way so that they can see the best course of action was the chosen one.

THIRTY-FIVE

Dealing with Passive-Aggressive Behavior

———⚉———

There are many different ways people can cause problems in teams and at work. One of the most common is undermining the team through passive-aggressive behavior. Stuck-in-the-Middle Management is rife with passive-aggressive individuals.

When you are a manager, there is no upside to passive-aggressive behavior. It is bad for you as a person and as a manager. Passive- aggressive behavior is bad for a team member and the team. It is bad for the work environment. Above all, passive-aggressive behavior is bad for the company.

What Is Passive-Aggressive Behavior?

Passive-aggressive people express negative feelings, resentment, and aggression in a passive, or indirect, way. They procrastinate. They deliberately fail to complete required work or tasks. Passive-aggressive behavior includes being stubborn, acting helpless, being manipulative, and showing resentment or sullenness.

I still remember working with Matthew, a team member who never said anything publicly when he disagreed with something. In one meeting for a new product launch, Matthew remained silent while all of the other team members spoke in agreement of the chosen path. I later learned that despite not speaking out, Matthew thought the product was flawed. He favored another product for which he had a central role in developing.

When it came time to work on the chosen product's launch, Matthew took steps to hinder the product's success. He routinely missed deadlines for his own work. He also held up other team member's work by not providing information and feedback in a timely manner and by being unhelpful.

Knowing the definition of passive-aggression is the easy part. Experts will tell you that passive-aggressive behavior is a defense mechanism that is often only partly conscious. *Your challenge as a manager is to recognize passive-aggressive behavior on the job and address the situation before it significantly affects your ability and that of your team to work productively.*

DEALING WITH PASSIVE-AGGRESSIVE BEHAVIOR

The first challenge is to *recognize passive-aggressive behavior for what it is.* That can take some time. People who are passive-aggressive often follow a pattern. Passive aggression tends to be an ongoing approach to dealing with things rather than a one-time or sporadic behavior. If someone is passive-aggressive in only one situation but does not behave that way in general, that individual may be reacting to something specific about the situation or something that is going on in his personal life.

If passive-aggressive behavior is an ongoing problem with someone, I recommend collecting at least three examples of this behavior and its impact on the team and general company operations. This will help you make your case and show that the behavior is not a one-time occurrence. As you collect this evidence, document the effect this behavior has on the team as a whole and the team's ability to adhere to its timelines.

With this information in hand, you can more confidently address the situation with the person involved, either directly or through that person's manager. If this approach does not solve the problem or result in a plan to solve it, you should be prepared to escalate the situation to someone higher in the organization.

In the end, you need to get yourself and your team as far away from this type of person as possible. When I covered this topic in a web episode on the *3 Minute Mentor* web site, I went as far as to say, *"Managers should fire passive-aggressive people."* That one idea caused more feedback that anything else I have said or written before or since.

One comment came from a self-described passive-aggressive person. That individual suggested that a manager should point out the passive-aggressive behavior, then remind the employee that it is important to be kind and welcoming. Of course, collecting and presenting evidence of this behavior is exactly the right thing to do, but that may not be what a passive-aggressive person wants to hear.

Another person suggested that managers should give people with passive-aggressive behavior more time to adjust to the situation. I am against giving passive-aggressive people extra help. Passive-aggression is not a disability to be reasonably accommodated. It is a habit that needs to be cut out from the workplace.

Managers need to take the time to work with passive-aggressive individuals. However, in a business, there is only so much managers can be expected to do. At some point, shareholders expect managers to deliver, not deliberate.

RECOGNIZING PASSIVE AGGRESSION IN YOURSELF

Much to my chagrin, I have found myself behaving passive-aggressively on the job.

As a manager, you too are not immune to passive-aggressive behavior. It just may be difficult for you to recognize it in yourself. *Anything you can do to prevent or eliminate passive aggression in your team or in your own behavior is important.*

If you are worried that you are being passive-aggressive, you can *guard against it by becoming more transparent in your decision-making.* Do not keep secrets. Do not remain silent when people want to know something.

Communicating when you are not going to do something is just as important as communicating when you are going to do something. Even though communicating about inaction is often more difficult than communicating about action, I still let people know my reasons for not doing something.

When you are transparent, you often reveal your motivation without saying anything. If your action or inaction is driven by dislike of a particular person or because you do not know what to do, this level of transparency will reveal those motivations.

Voluntary transparency allows you to identify problems in your decision-making so that you can address those problems. It also allows you to identify when you have made the right choice and the reasons behind that choice.

In some cases, when I have done this, someone on my team has escalated my decisions. I recognize the risk of that happening, and the fact that my decision not to do something may be reversed by someone higher up.

In every situation, I organize my reasons for my decision and communicate them when necessary. If I believe an action is the wrong thing to do and someone uses analysis and quantified data to prove that the action is the right thing to do, I have to have the integrity to own up to my miscalculation and move forward. In these cases, even if you make a bad decision that is ultimately reversed, people will still respect you for your honesty and integrity in handling the situation.

The Bottom Line

» There is no upside to passive-aggressive behavior.

Next Steps

1. Think through who on your team or in your work environment exhibits passive-aggressive behavior. *Do you exhibit it yourself?* Commit to working with those identified to eliminate this bad habit.

2. Next time you find yourself in a meeting where you do not want to do something that everyone seems

in support of, speak up, carefully and cautiously. Outline your rationale.

3. If, as a manager, you have identified a team member who ignores your requests to scuttle his or her passive-aggressive behavior, consider whether to fire that person.

THIRTY-SIX

MANAGING DIVERSITY

As an Englishman, I was unfamiliar with diversity as a business issue when I first moved to the United States in 1996. However, that soon changed. In fact, diversity was among the initial list of new business terms I learned when I began working for an American company. Diversity was certainly an important issue at that time in the United Kingdom, but I am not sure we had the same amount of organization or structure around it.

Over the years, I have seen the importance of diversity for businesses and for people. As an employee and manager, it is important for you to understand diversity and its role in managing a business.

Ineffective Stuck-in-the-Middle Managers may not see the importance of diversity, and may be unwilling to take steps to increase diversity.

WHAT IS DIVERSITY?

Too much cynicism exists around diversity. Much of this stems from a stereotyping of diversity as a way to be "PC" or politically correct. We should be clear at work that diversity is not about political correctness. It is also less about quotas or affirmative action, although some government laws and regulations do come into play. True diversity is more than just common decency to those around you, although that is an important part of it.

Diversity involves making sure that your business reflects the markets you live in. It is about maintaining your employee base as diverse as your labor market and your customer base.

In a global marketplace, diversity makes a great deal of business sense. Your people—men and women of all generations from all types of ethnic and racial backgrounds—should reflect the markets in which you operate and in which you sell your products and services. If you run a diverse business, you are more likely to have the respect of your customers and business partners. Some of those organizations, including government entities, evaluate levels of diversity when choosing vendors and business partners.

WHY DOES DIVERSITY MATTER?

There are many reasons why diversity is important. Some of these reasons are driven by business sense and some may be driven by government regulation. In our At Work survey, nearly half of the people we surveyed did not understand or know how to value diversity at work, and only one-third thought diversity helps them get promoted at work. The implication is that while diversity is important, we all have a responsibility to articulate its value.

Let's first focus on the business reasons for diversity. When you have a diverse workforce, it changes the way people in the company think and work. In a diverse workplace, you are more likely to be around different types of people who can introduce new approaches at work. People from different cultures and backgrounds often bring unexpected and fresh perspectives to problem solving, design, and product development.

Some people are more analytical while others are more creative. People from varying religious, political, and socioeconomic backgrounds possess different perspectives on the world and specific issues. Bring all of these types of people together and you are likely to see more creativity, new and better ideas, and more innovation.

Numerous examples exist in the business world where diversity generated a significant financial windfall. One of the most famous cases occurred when a group of Hispanics at Frito-Lay in the U.S. (part of PepsiCo) suggested the company develop a Guacamole Chip. That chip generated $100 million in sales in its first year.[1]

I do not believe that a company can truly understand its markets without a diverse workforce. Those who analyze these markets need to empathize with the markets and customers in order to make good decisions on how to approach and interact with them.

A company moving into new global markets in predominantly Muslim countries or Asian countries needs to rethink its marketing approaches, communications, and overall imagery. If the company's marketing graphics and images continue to feature white, middle-aged men and women wearing crosses around their necks, the company's appeal in those markets will be limited.

A company selling women's clothing targeted to a market made up of Hispanic women between the ages of fifteen and twenty-nine better have Hispanic women in that age bracket on staff to manage that process. Similarly, an equipment company that manufactures machinery for golf course construction and maintenance not only needs people with the technical knowledge necessary to sell that equipment, but also people

---

1 Taken from *Management* by Chuck Williams

who play golf themselves and understand the importance of, and what is required for, a well-maintained course.

Don't overlook the importance of age diversity in the workplace. Some people dislike hiring young people. Others are uncomfortable hiring people older than them. The argument goes that the young are too inexperienced and the old are more difficult to manage or don't have the skills and insight necessary to succeed in today's workplace. While it is important to employ people who look like your market, it is also important to employ people who are right for the job. Making judgments based on someone's age rather than on facts, even refusing to meet with people over a certain age, is prejudice pure and simple. That is no way to form a team.

In some countries or communities, government or legal issues require you to think through your diversity policies. In most cases, governments do not force quotas on your business. Instead, you will likely have to prove your company's diverse workforce if you are to win government business. Both local and federal authorities want assurance that the company has a diverse racial and ethnic population, plus a significant percentage of women in senior positions. They may even review your company's support and enablement of disabled people in the workforce. Failure to manage to these criteria may limit or exclude you from certain business opportunities.

There are certain countries and communities that enforce diversity on a workforce and on company ownership. If you want to do business in one of these areas, you should seek legal counsel to work through those issues.

What Is the Best Approach to Diversity?

A company's approach to diversity will depend on its size. A company with thousands or even tens of thousands of employees can more easily establish targets for diversity-hiring based on race, ethnicity, ability, and age. These targets can be tracked and managed by the Human Resources department and reported out at team and departmental levels. If you work in an environment like this, it is important to be supportive of the company's diversity practices and procedures. There is little benefit to be gained from resisting or fighting these policies.

In a large company with, say, one thousand executives, it is much easier to open up opportunities to specific groups to enhance diversity. If half of those executives are not women, it is important to consider why that is, and to take steps to address it.

Ensuring diversity in smaller teams within a large company can be difficult. In such cases, it is important not to force or mandate diversity. Diversity is even more difficult for a small business that does limited hiring. Even so, these companies should do their best to make sure that their employee demographics reflect the customer base.

You need to make a conscious decision to support, enable, and celebrate diversity. Your efforts will be visible to those around you based on what you say, how you say it, and what you do. Whether you are a second-line manager or a senior executive, people notice if you review the diversity of your frontline or first-level teams. Just asking the question, "Did you consider any minority candidates for this role?" can set the right tone with your team.

One of the best ways to improve diversity is through recruitment. Small changes when targeting job advertising and where the company gleans applications, such as job fairs and universities, can improve diversity by providing a more diverse pool of potential hires. If you only go to one place, like an Ivy League school, to get new recruits, you are only ever going to hire one type of person. Even carefully considering who should conduct interviews for specific positions can help to increase diversity.

THE BOTTOM LINE

» Diversity may be "the right thing to do"—but it is also the right thing to do *for the business.*

NEXT STEPS

1. Review, with your Human Resources team, where the company advertises job openings, and come up with new ideas that could increase the pool of diverse candidates.

2. Ask the Human Resources team if they can get a speaker at your next team meeting to talk about the role diversity has in helping businesses improve performance and accelerate your business.

3. If the makeup of your team is not diverse, use any upcoming and unanticipated job openings as an opportunity to bring in those more apt to understand, empathize with, and be members of the ideal customer base.

KEY SKILLS TO BE A 21ST CENTURY EXECUTIVE

I have devoted the previous thirty-six chapters to giving advice on how to avoid being a Stuck-in-the-Middle Manager, and how to start behaving like (and becoming) a 21st Century Executive. Like most people, I have received a lot of advice in my career. Some of it has been helpful and memorable, and some of it has not. I have channeled the best of this advice into this book.

When I speak in public as the 3 Minute Mentor, people often ask for the best general advice I have to give. The reality is that most of the material I use as the 3 Minute Mentor is either a variation on common sense or based on what I have learned from others.

The real key to breaking away from the pack is *knowing how to learn from others who are generous enough to share their advice and experiences.* Therefore, I would like to end this book by sharing with you three of the most important pieces of advice I have received during my career.

1. YOU CAN'T HAVE IT ALL.

There is always a lot of talk about work/life balance. This usually takes the form of articles in business magazines that feature senior executives or consultants who run high-powered corporate divisions and still find time to run marathons, feed the hungry, and raise ten children.

While these people certainly exist, most of us cannot do it all—and those people probably do not either. They, like the rest of us, have to make compromises and choices in their lives.

Life is less about balance than about choices. In your career, you will face a constant barrage of choices that will, in turn, affect the rest of your life. You can choose to do a job you love that does not pay very much. You can choose to spend long hours in the office instead of with your family or vice versa. In either case, *the choice you make in one part of your life will have significant implications for the other parts.*

If you work late nights and weekends, that is your choice, and that choice is likely to pay dividends in terms of career progression and financial rewards. If you are not willing to put in that time and you work for a company that expects that level of sacrifice and commitment, you need either to accept that, or to move on to a company or position that provides a less stark choice.

Keep in mind that *these choices are not static.* You may need to focus on work at certain points in time, and on your personal life at other times.

One of my best bosses spent her time making smart choices in building a career. This executive long focused on work and career issues, until family matters required her attention. At that point, she decided to put work on hold and take a sabbatical to help her aging mother. She is still someone I respect today. She made the right choices for her family and her life.

If you choose family over work, you may not get promoted. If you choose work over family, that may have a negative effect on your family relationships.

In my experience, *failure to take responsibility for your choices almost always leads to negativity.* I have met many people who are content to just let things happen in life and in their careers. If you are content to let things work themselves out and you are happy with the outcome of that approach, more power to you. However, make sure that this and everything else that you do is a result of *your own conscious choices.* If things do not work out well, you have no one to blame but yourself for not taking the right steps or preparing appropriately.

2. KNOW YOUR END GAME.

In Chapter 1 of this book, we looked at career planning. It may seem strange that I reemphasize this at the end of the book, too. Remember: *your end game will become a defining thought in your work life.*

When it comes to your career, you need to have a clear sense of where you are going. All of your choices should be made with that end game in mind.

One friend focused his career on making a certain amount of money and achieving a certain level in the corporate world before leaving it all behind to work in the nonprofit sector. He focused his career moves on achieving that outcome, and it was his choice to do so. For others, making money and retiring early to the golf course was a more important goal than working for a nonprofit organization.

Some people focus their end game on making time for their family. If family is more important to you than career advancement, that will influence your end game and determine what choices you make and how you make them.

When I left my last role, one of the e-mails wishing me well came from Bob, a colleague who had left the same company some time before me. Bob told me what a good decision it was for him to leave the company, and I agreed with him. We also recalled a dinner we had had in New York when he asked me for some career advice. He wanted to be an executive responsible for running a team, and he was worried that it had not yet happened, and perhaps never would. At age forty, Bob was concerned that he wasn't where he thought he would be. He was having what I sometimes call a "midcareer crisis."

This crisis often happens around about the age of forty, which is about the career midpoint for most people. You hit forty and look at where you are and what lies ahead. If your reality doesn't match what you planned twenty years ago, the reason why invariably ties back to your choices and decisions.

We are where we are because of the roles we chose, the family commitments we honored, and even the fact that we like the city where we are living and do not want to move. None of these decisions and choices are wrong—but they do affect your career.

My advice to Bob was simple. If he wanted to be an executive and run a bigger team, he needed to reset his career destination. At the same time, he had to be aware of the trade-offs involved. It is never too late to make new choices, but we often have to consider the others in our family when we make those choices.

3. REMEMBER THAT YOU NEED
TO LIVE WITH YOUR CONSCIENCE.

I received this third piece of advice from a British expatriate while having dinner at his hillside restaurant on the Spanish island of Majorca. His advice was simple: *make every decision with your head, and execute it with your heart.*

I do not remember how this conversation came up or why he told me this, but it is one of those things that stay with you. I try to live it every day. Each night as I put my head on my pillow, I ask myself whether I followed that advice on that day.

You can follow this advice, too. We all know that making strong business decisions can be a very difficult part of our lives.

The hardest decisions you need to make as a manager or senior executive involve layoffs. As someone who sits at the "head table" during that discussion, I have had to decide not only whether to okay layoffs, but how many and in what areas. If you aspire to a leadership role, you will face these types of decisions, too. You may even be called on to take a larger sacrifice for your area of the business.

As a businessperson, you know you need to be able to make those decisions based on business data and facts. You understand that the good of the many sometimes outweighs the good of the few. You understand the need to make hard decisions and that you often have no other choice. *And although you may have no control over the decision itself, you do have control over how you carry it out.*

Managing how we act following a difficult decision is what makes it easier to sleep at night. How will we put a severance package together? How will we communicate that to people? How can we handle this situation with respect instead of hiding? *This is the time to use our hearts....*

Executing decisions with heart is not easy. Those around you may argue with your judgment. Some individuals may balk at providing a bit more to the people being laid off. Or they may want to save a few dollars by making the payouts all at once rather than spreading them out (which would be more tax-efficient for those laid off).

Although you cannot win all of these battles, you can think carefully about these potential situations beforehand to decide which ones to fight and how. You can also think through your own behavior. In this situation, the hardest part is delivering the news. Did you look people in the eye? Did you treat them with respect? Even if you are the only one who remembers your actions, that is still important because you will know and must live with how you acted.

You work to live, as they say.

I say, do it with heart and dignity.

NIGEL DESSAU

Nigel Dessau describes himself as a longtime professional marketer. He has worked in the frontline trenches of marketing, plodded his way through middle management, and reached the executive level, including the position of chief marketing officer.

Nigel is the creator and driving force behind the *3 Minute Mentor* website. This website provides significant yet simple, easy-to-follow career guidance in three-minute videos. The website claims thousands of subscribers from all over the world. *Become a 21st Century Executive: Breaking Away from the Pack* is based upon episodes and concepts found in the *3 Minute Mentor (www.3minutementor.com)*.

Over his twenty-five-years-plus career, Dessau has held almost every job level in companies big and small. He began his career by working for IBM in the British town of Basingstoke. For his first ten years at IBM, Nigel served customers and partners in the UK. Following an assignment to Poughkeepsie, New York, Dessau decided to move to the US, where he continued to work for IBM. During those nine years with IBM in the US, Nigel worked on such diverse projects as the worldwide launch of IBM eServer zSeries and then headed up the marketing programs for the S/390 brand. As part of the corporate marketing team,

Dessau led the marketing strategy behind e-business as well as the transition to On Demand Business.

Since leaving IBM, Nigel has held senior executive and CMO roles at StorageTek, Sun Microsystems, AMD, and Stratus Technologies.

Born and educated in Nottingham, England, Nigel lives with his wife in Boston, MA.

Contact Nigel by e-mail at *contact@the3minutementor.com.*

Visit the companion website for this book:
www.the3minutementor.com

Thank you for reading
*Become a 21st Century Executive:
Breaking Away from the Pack.*

Share your comments at:
www.the3minutementor.com

CPSIA information can be obtained at www.ICGtesting.com
Printed in the USA
BVOW03s1056070515

399304BV00003B/6/P